THE ADVENTURES OF LUNA THE RESCUE CAT

Luna B

Copyright 2024

All rights reserved. No part of this book may be reproduced or transmitted in any form or means without permission from the authors.

Luna

1

Once upon a time there was a beautiful sleek black cat with sparkling green eyes called Luna who patiently sat in her cozy corner of the Evesham cat adoption centre. She wished for a forever home, and today she felt a buzz of excitement in the air. Luna's green eyes sparkled with hope as she watched the visitors come and go, each one bringing hope of a new family.

Luna had heard whispers among the staff about a couple named Pete and Susie who were looking for a cat to adopt. They were supposed to visit today, and Luna could not help but feel a flutter of anticipation. She wanted to make a good impression.

As the front door opened, a cheerful voice rang out: "Look at all these lovely cats!" Susie exclaimed, her eyes shining with delight. Pete, standing beside her, smiled warmly as his eyes surveyed the room.

Luna stood up and stretched, shaking out her fur. She knew this was her moment. With a confident flick of her tail, she trotted over to the pair, ready to charm them with her playful spirit.

"Hey there, little one," Pete said, as he knelt to meet Luna's gaze. "Aren't you a beauty?"

Luna purred, rubbing against his hand. This was going well! Susie knelt beside Pete, her face lighting up as she reached out to pet Luna. "I love her! She is so friendly!"

The shelter staff introduced Luna, sharing her story of resilience and her journey as a rescue cat. "She's got a wonderful personality," they said. "She loves to play and is quite the little explorer."

Luna seized the moment, playfully swatting at a nearby feather toy. She bounded around, showing off her agility and charm, her little paws dancing with excitement. Pete and Susie laughed, clearly smitten.

Just then, a voice chimed in: "Is this the cat you're thinking of adopting?"- it was Daphne, Pete's mum, who had come along for support.

"Oh, yes!" Susie replied. "Look how sweet she is!"

Daphne smiled, leaning down to give Luna some gentle scratches behind her ears. "I think she is perfect for you. You all will have so much fun together."

Luna soaked up the attention, her heart swelling with happiness. She loved being around people, and the thought of being part of a family filled her with joy.

After a few more minutes of playing and getting to know one another, Pete and Susie exchanged excited glances.

"We'd love to adopt her!" Pete said, grinning widely. "Luna is the one!"

The staff helped them with the adoption paperwork, and Luna could hardly contain her excitement. She was finally going to have a forever home! As they prepared to leave, Luna felt a warmth wrapping around her and had the sense of belonging that she had always dreamed of.

When everything was settled, Susie gently scooped Luna into her arms. "Welcome to the family, Luna!" she said, her voice full of warmth.

Luna purred happily, snuggling into Susie's embrace. Pete smiled and added, "We can't wait to introduce you to your new home."

As they left the shelter, Luna peeked out from Susie's arms, feeling a mix of excitement and comfort. She could not wait to explore her new surroundings, meet new friends, and create wonderful memories with Pete, Susie, and Daphne.

On the way home, they talked about all the adventures they would share together. Luna imagined cozy evenings on the sofa, sunny spots for napping, and lots of playtime with her new family.

When they arrived home, Luna stepped down from Susie's arms, her paws touching the soft carpet for the first time. She sniffed the air, taking in the scents of her new space. It felt warm and inviting, and she knew she was exactly where she belonged.

With a joyful flick of her tail, Luna explored her new home- her heart full of hope and happiness. She had waited patiently to be adopted, and now her dreams had come true. Luna was ready to fill her new family's lives with love, laughter, and the spirit of adventure that only a rescue cat could bring.

2

One morning, Luna heard the news that her friend Norman Jones had opened a new radio station called *Topcat Radio*, and she could not wait to check it out. The buzz around town was that it featured all kinds of music, stories, and even a segment for pet advice!

As Luna padded through the charming streets, she imagined all the fun she would have at the station. When she arrived, the building was decorated with colourful banners and a big sign that read *Topcat Radio*. Luna's tail flicked with excitement as she stepped inside.

The station was lively, with music playing softly in the background and the sound of voices bustling about. Norman, a cheerful man with a friendly smile, was busy setting up his equipment when he spotted Luna. "Luna! I am so glad you came!" he exclaimed, waving her over.

"Hi, Norman! I am excited to see your new station!" Luna meowed; her green eyes sparkling.

"Welcome to Topcat Radio!" Norman said, gesturing around. "We have got a lot going on today. Would you like to join me for a live segment? I think our listeners would love to hear from you!"

Luna's ears perked up at the idea. "Really? I would love to!"

They headed into the cozy studio, filled with microphones, soundboards, and colourful posters. Norman adjusted his headphones and welcomed the audience. "Hello, everyone! You are listening to Topcat Radio, and today we have a special guest- Luna the rescue cat! Let us hear what she has to say!"

Luna felt a little nervous but also excited. She took a deep breath and began to share her thoughts about the joys of being a rescue cat, the importance of adoption, and how pets can brighten a home. "It's wonderful to find a forever family," she meowed with warmth and sincerity.

The listeners were captivated. Norman chimed in with questions, asking about Luna's favourite adventures and her friends in town. They chatted about everything from the best places to nap to the importance of playtime.

"Do you have any advice for our listeners?" Norman asked, grinning. Luna thought for a moment. "Always take time to explore and have fun! Whether it is chasing a feather or finding a sunny spot, every day is an adventure."

After the segment, Norman clapped his hands in excitement. "That was amazing, Luna! You really connected with our audience. How about we play some of your favourite songs next?"

"Oh, yes please! I love music!" Luna meowed enthusiastically.

Norman queued up some upbeat tunes, and they danced around the studio, Luna twirling and leaping to the rhythm. The energy was infectious, and soon they were both laughing and enjoying the moment.

As the day went on, Luna helped Norman with other segments, including a pet care advice part where they answered listener questions about taking care of cats and dogs. She felt proud to contribute to something that could help others.

Before the day ended, Norman surprised Luna with a special treat. He had created a slot just for her called 'Luna's Corner,' where she could share her adventures and thoughts every week. "You'll be our resident expert on all things feline!" he declared.

Luna beamed with joy. "Thank you so much, Norman! I cannot wait to share more stories!"

As she left the station, Luna felt a warm glow in her heart. She had not only enjoyed a fantastic day at Topcat Radio but had also formed a new bond with Norman and the community of listeners.

Walking home, Luna envisioned all the adventures she would share in her new radio segment, knowing that every story would bring joy to those who tuned in. With a happy flick of her tail, she looked forward to her next visit to the station, ready to inspire and entertain once more.

3

One autumn evening, Luna met with her friends Paul and Lisa who had invited her to join them on a ghost hunting expedition at an old, haunted mansion on the outskirts of town. Luna loved a good mystery, and the idea of exploring spooky places with her friends thrilled her.

As the sun began to set, casting long shadows and painting the sky with hues of orange and purple, Luna trotted over to meet Paul and Lisa. They were equipped with flashlights, a camera and notebook to jot down any spooky encounters.

"Are you ready for a night of ghostly adventures?" Paul asked with a grin.

"Absolutely!" Luna replied, her green eyes sparkling with excitement. "Let's see if we can find any friendly spirits!"

The trio made their way to the mansion, which loomed eerily against the twilight sky. Its creaky wooden doors and overgrown garden gave it an air of mystery. As they approached, Lisa read aloud from her notes about the mansion's history. "Legend has it that a kind-hearted woman once lived here, and her spirit still watches over the place."

"Maybe we'll get to meet her!" Luna replied, her tail twitching with excitement.

Inside, the air was cool and filled with the scent of old wood and dust. They shone their flashlights around the dimly lit rooms, revealing cobwebs and faded photographs of the mansion's former inhabitants. Luna felt a shiver of excitement run down her spine.

As they explored, Lisa said: "We can ask questions and see if we get any responses!"- as she began setting up a small recorder.

They gathered in a circle, and Paul began: "Is there anyone here with us? If you can hear us, please make a noise."

The room fell silent, and Luna's ears perked up, listening intently. After a few moments, they heard a soft rustle, as if someone or something was moving in the shadows.

"Did you hear that?" Luna whispered, her heart racing.

Lisa nodded- her eyes wide with excitement: "Let's try again!"

They asked more questions, and this time they heard a faint whisper, almost like a gentle sigh. Paul played back the recording, and they all leaned in to listen closely. "What do you think it said?" he asked, intrigued.

"I think it sounded like 'help'," Luna meowed, her voice low. "Maybe the spirit wants to share something with us."

Feeling a mix of curiosity and determination, they decided to continue exploring. They made their way to the grand staircase, which creaked under their weight. As they reached the top, they found a dusty old room filled with forgotten treasures: a mirror, a trunk, and even an antique rocking chair.

Suddenly, the chair began to rock slowly, even though there was no breeze. Luna's fur stood on end, but she felt a strange sense of comfort. "I think she's trying to communicate!" she said in a steady voice.

Paul and Lisa watched in awe. "This is incredible!" Paul exclaimed. "What should we do next?"

"Maybe we should ask her about her story" Lisa suggested. "She might want us to know something important."

They gathered around the rocking chair and asked: "Can you tell us your name? We would love to hear your story."

As if in response, the air grew still, and they felt a gentle warmth enveloping them. A soft voice, almost like a whisper, echoed in the room. It was faint but clear: "Emily."

"Emily!" Luna repeated, feeling a connection to the spirit. "What happened to you?"

There was another whisper, "Love... lost... found."

The trio exchanged glances, touched by the message. They could sense Emily's kindness and the lingering love she had for her home. Lisa spoke softly: "We are here to listen. You are not alone anymore."

Feeling a wave of calm wash over them, they realized they were part of something special. Emily's spirit had found a way to connect with them, sharing a piece of her history and reminding them of the love that can endure even beyond life.

As the night wore on, they continued to explore and share stories, feeling a bond with Emily and one another. By the time they left the mansion, Luna felt a deep sense of fulfilment. They had not only gone ghost hunting but had also made a connection with a spirit that had a story to tell.

With a happy flick of her tail, Luna trotted home, excited to share their adventure with her friends, and eager for more explorations in the future. She knew that the mysteries of the past could be as beautiful and heartwarming as the friendships she cherished in her life.

4

Luna awoke to the sound of bustling activity in her home. She stretched her paws and padded into the living room, where her human mum, Susie, was packing a suitcase. "Good morning, Luna! Guess what?" Susie said, her eyes sparkling with excitement, "We're going on holiday!"

Luna's ears perked up. "A holiday? Where are we going?" she meowed, intrigued.

Susie smiled. "We are going to a lovely seaside town for a week! You will get to explore new places, feel the sand under your paws, and enjoy the fresh sea air."

Luna could not believe her ears! She loved the idea of new adventures. "That sounds amazing! But what about my cozy window perch?" she meowed with a hint of concern. "Do not worry, Luna! We will bring your favourite blanket and some toys. You will have everything you need," Susie reassured her.

After a busy morning of packing, they hopped into the car, and Luna settled in her travel carrier, her heart racing with

excitement. As they drove, she watched the scenery change from familiar streets to open fields and eventually to the sparkling blue ocean in the distance.

When they finally arrived at their seaside cottage, Luna could hardly contain her excitement. The salty breeze filled the air, and she jumped out of her carrier, ready to explore. Susie opened the door, and Luna bounded inside, her paws padding on the wooden floor.

The cottage was cozy and bright, with windows that overlooked the beach. Luna quickly found her favourite blanket in her suitcase and claimed a sunny spot by the window. "This is perfect!" she purred contentedly.

After settling in, Susie said: "Let's go explore the beach!" Luna's eyes lit up at the idea. They made their way down to the sandy shore, where the sound of waves crashing filled the air. Luna felt the warm sand under her paws for the first time. She danced around, her tail flicking with joy.

The beach was full of new sights and sounds. Seagulls called overhead, and families were playing nearby. Luna spotted a group of children building something with sand and she curiously approached. "Hello! What are you making?" she meowed.

"We're building a castle!" one of the kids exclaimed, grinning. "Do you want to help?"

Luna could not resist. She joined in the fun, playfully patting the sand with her paws while the children added seashells as decorations. They laughed and cheered, and Luna felt like part of the team.

After the sandcastle was complete, Luna and Susie took a leisurely stroll along the shoreline. They collected seashells and watched the waves roll in and out. Luna loved the sound of the water and the feeling of the gentle breeze in her fur.

As the sun began to set, painting the sky with shades of pink and orange, they headed back to the cottage. Luna curled up on her blanket, feeling blissfully happy and a little tired from all the excitement of the day.

That night, as they settled in, Susie said: "We have so many adventures planned for this week, Luna. You are going to love it!"

Luna purred softly, dreaming of all the fun they would have- more trips to the beach, exploring tide pools, and maybe even chasing some crabs. The next morning, Luna woke to the sound of waves crashing and the sun streaming through the windows.

With a stretch and a yawn, she was ready for another day of adventure. Holidaying by the sea was everything she had dreamed of and more.

5

One sunny afternoon, Luna decided to explore the garden. As she ventured out, she spotted June her neighbour, and her energetic dog, Archie, playing fetch.

Archie, a large friendly boxer, immediately noticed Luna and bounded over, tail wagging excitedly. Luna, unsure of this large creature, puffed up her fur and arched her back slightly, ready to make a hasty retreat. But June knelt, gently calling out: "Hey there, Luna! It is okay, he is friendly!"

With June's soothing voice, Luna hesitated, intrigued. Archie, sensing her hesitation, dropped his toy and sat down, his big brown eyes watching her with curiosity and kindness. "I am Archie, I will not hurt you. Do you want to play" he barked loudly.

After a moment, Luna took a cautious step forward, her whiskers twitching in curiosity.

June smiled as she watched the two slowly inch closer. Archie's playful spirit seemed to put Luna at ease, and soon enough, she was sniffing around him, her tail flicking with

newfound confidence. They may have been different sizes but they became great friends.

6

On a chilly Halloween evening, Luna was buzzing with excitement. This year, she was going trick-or-treating for the very first time, with her friends Blinky, Rosco, Bob, and Apollo by her side. They all wore their best costumes, ready to explore the neighbourhood together.

Luna had chosen a cute pumpkin outfit, complete with a little green hat that sat jauntily on her head. Blinky- a fluffy tabby cat- was dressed as a little ghost, with a white sheet that billowed around her. Rosco- a scrappy, playful orange cat- was a pirate, complete with a tiny eye patch and a makeshift sword. Bob, the wise elder of the group, had decided to go as a wizard, complete with a sparkly hat. Finally, Apollo- a black sleek and charming cat- was a dashing vampire with a tiny cape that fluttered as he walked.

"Ready for some fun?" Luna meowed, her eyes sparkling with excitement as they gathered outside. "Absolutely!" Blinky said, bouncing on her paws. "I can't wait to collect all the treats!"

As the sun dipped below the horizon, they set off down the street, filled with excitement. The neighbourhood was a swirl of decorations- glowing pumpkins, cobwebs draped over bushes, and skeletons dancing in front yards. It felt magical.

Their first stop was at the house of their friend Theresa, who opened the door with a smile. "Look at you all! You look fantastic!" she exclaimed, reaching down to give each of them a gentle pat.

"Trick or treat!" they chorused, their meows filled with excitement.

As she dropped treats into their bags, Luna felt a warm glow of joy. This was everything she had hoped it would be!

They wandered from house to house, each stop filled with laughter and delight. Luna loved seeing her friends in their costumes, and they all encouraged each other to be brave and visit the spookier houses.

"Let's try that one!" Rosco said, pointing to a house decorated with eerie lights and a fog machine. "It looks awesome!"

"Are we sure about this?" Blinky asked, her voice trembling slightly.

"Of course! Together, we can do anything!" Apollo said, puffing out his chest. They approached the spooky house. Luna tapped her paw on the door, her heart racing. The door creaked open, revealing a friendly neighbour in a silly monster costume. "Trick or treat!" the cats exclaimed, their nerves turning into laughter.

The neighbour laughed and filled their bags with extra goodies. "You all look great! Enjoy your night!"

As they moved on, Luna felt a sense of belonging. It was wonderful to share this adventure with her friends, and they made each other braver with every house they visited.

After a while, they reached the park where a Halloween festival was taking place. Colourful lights twinkled in the trees, and there were games and activities. "Let's check it out!" Bob suggested, his wizard hat wobbling as he walked.

They played games, won more treats, and even joined in a friendly cat costume contest. Luna felt proud as they all cheered for one another, their friendship shining through. As the evening wound down, they decided to head home, their bags heavy with goodies. Luna could not stop smiling and her heart was filled with happiness. "This was the best Halloween ever!" she exclaimed.

"I can't believe how much fun we had," Blinky agreed, her ghostly sheet billowing as she bounced along.

Back home again, Luna snuggled up with her friends, each cat sharing their favourite moments of the night. As they counted their treats and shared stories, Luna knew this was a Halloween she would never forget.

With a full belly and a happy heart, Luna purred contentedly, feeling grateful for the wonderful adventures she had shared with her friends. Halloween had brought them closer together, and she could not wait for the next adventure they would embark on.

7

One bright afternoon, Luna heard the familiar sound of her human friend Daphne bustling around in the bathroom. Luna was always curious about what Daphne was up to, especially when it involved beauty products and fun colours.

Suddenly, Daphne called out: "Luna, come here! You are going to love this!"

Intrigued, Luna hopped off the windowsill and padded into the bathroom. There, she saw Daphne holding a box with vibrant colours and a big smile on her face. "I decided it is time for a change! I am going to dye my hair a beautiful shade of purple!"

Luna's eyes widened in excitement. She had seen Daphne experiment with different colours before, but purple was a new choice. "That sounds fantastic!" Luna purred, imagining how stunning Daphne would look.

As Daphne set up her supplies, Luna found a cozy spot on a towel nearby, ready to supervise the process. She watched

closely as Daphne carefully mixed the dye and applied it to her hair.

"This is going to be so much fun!" Daphne exclaimed, laughing a little as she splattered some dye on her forehead.

Luna could not help but chuckle, her tail flicking with amusement.

After a little time, Daphne rinsed her hair and carefully dried it off. Luna's anticipation grew as Daphne revealed the final look. With a flourish, Daphne turned to the mirror and styled her newly coloured hair. The purple was vibrant and beautiful, shimmering in the light.

"Ta-da! What do you think, Luna?" Daphne asked, her eyes sparkling with joy.

Luna hopped up on the bathroom counter, getting a closer look. "You look amazing, Daphne! The purple suits you perfectly!"

Daphne grinned and twirled around playfully. "I feel like a whole new person! I cannot wait to show everyone!"

Excited to help her celebrate her new look, Luna suggested: "Let us go for a walk! You can show off your fabulous hair to the neighbours." With a playful nod, Daphne grabbed her bag, and they headed out together. As they walked through the neighbourhood, Luna trotted beside Daphne, her tail

held high in pride. Everyone they passed could not help but compliment Daphne on her striking new hair colour.

"Wow, you look fantastic!" one neighbour called out. "That purple really pops!"

As they continued their walk, they stopped by the park, where Luna could chase some butterflies while Daphne chatted with friends.

That evening, as they settled down together at home, Luna curled up in Daphnes lap. "I love your new hair, Daphne. It makes you even more beautiful."

Daphne smiled, gently stroking Luna's fur. "Thank you, I am so glad you are here to share this with me."

With that, they both relaxed, enjoying the rest of the evening together.

8

Luna was sitting on the windowsill when she noticed her friend Peter, a local photographer, rushing down the street with a look of panic on his face. Luna could tell something was wrong. She leapt down and decided to follow him. "Peter! What is the matter?" she meowed, trotting beside him. "Oh, Luna!" Peter exclaimed, stopping in his tracks, "I have lost my cameras! I had them with me while I was taking photos at the park, and now I cannot find them anywhere!"

Luna's heart sank for her friend. She knew how much Peter loved his cameras; they were his tools for capturing the beauty of the world. "Don't worry, I'll help you find them!" she said, her tail flicking with determination. With renewed energy, Peter and Luna headed to the park, retracing his steps. As they arrived, the vibrant green grass and colourful flowers greeted them, but Peter's cameras were nowhere to be seen.

"Let's think," Peter said, scratching his head, "I remember sitting on a bench near the big oak tree. Maybe I left them there!"

They quickly made their way to the bench. Luna jumped onto the seat, sniffing around for any clues. But as they looked, there were no cameras to be found.

"Maybe I dropped them on the way to the fountain!" Peter suggested, looking worried.

With Luna leading the way, they dashed to the fountain, where children splashed and laughed. Luna scanned the area, her sharp eyes searching everywhere. They checked behind the fountain and under nearby benches, but still no cameras. "Let's try the trail by the flower garden," Luna suggested. "You might have left them there while taking pictures of the flowers."

Nodding, Peter followed her as they hurried down the winding path. They arrived at the flower garden, its vibrant colours in full bloom. Luna weaved through the flowers, her nose twitching with excitement. Suddenly, she spotted something shiny, half-hidden among the petals. "There!" Luna meowed, bounding over to the colourful patch. She reached the spot and nudged the object with her paw- it was Peter's camera!

"Great job, Luna!" Pete exclaimed, rushing over. "That is one of them! But where is the other?"

"Let us check the picnic area. You might have set it down while you were eating." They dashed to the picnic area, where families were enjoying their meals. Luna and Peter

scanned the area, hoping to find the second camera. Just as Peter was starting to feel hopeless, Luna spotted a familiar strap peeking out from behind a nearby picnic blanket.

"There it is!" she meowed, running over. Peter followed, and they both reached the blanket at the same time.

"Thank goodness!" Peter said, picking up the second camera with a relieved smile. "You found them both, Luna! I could not have done it without you."

Luna purred happily, her green eyes shining with pride. "I am glad I could help! Now you can capture all the beautiful moments again."

With his cameras safely in hand, Peter grinned and ruffled Luna's fur affectionately. "Let us celebrate! How about a photo shoot together? I will take some pictures of you, my favourite feline helper."

Luna's eyes lit up. "That sounds wonderful!"

As they found a sunny spot in the park, Peter set up his camera and captured Luna in all her playful poses: sitting, pouncing, and even lounging on a sun-drenched rock. With every click, Luna felt happier, knowing she had helped her friend.

After the photoshoot, they shared a delightful picnic of treats Peter had packed. Luna enjoyed every moment, knowing that their friendship had grown stronger through

this little adventure. Together, they laughed, played, and made memories- one snapshot at a time.

9

Luna was out for her usual stroll when she spotted something that made her heart sink. Her favourite tree, a grand old oak that provided shade and a perfect napping spot, was marked with a bright red "X." It looked like it was in danger of being cut down!

Luna knew she had to do something. She remembered her friend, Councillor Anne, who always cared about the community and the environment- plus, Anne had a lovely cat named Apollo who was always up for a chat. Luna decided to pay them a visit.

With determination, Luna trotted down the familiar path to Anne's office. As she approached, she saw Anne sitting at her desk, busy with paperwork. When she spotted Luna, her face lit up. "Luna! What a lovely surprise!" she said, bending down to scratch behind Luna's ears. "What brings you here today?"

Luna meowed softly, trying to convey her urgency. "It is about the old oak tree by the park. It is marked for removal! We must save it!"

Anne's eyes widened with concern. "Oh no! That tree is so important to the community. It provides shade, homes for birds, and a beautiful place for everyone to enjoy.

Let us see what we can do!"

Just then, Apollo sauntered into the room, his fluffy tail held high. "What's all the commotion about?" he meowed, looking curiously at Luna and Anne.

Luna quickly explained the situation to Apollo. "We must save the tree! It is a special place for everyone, and I love napping there."

Apollo nodded wisely. "Let us rally some support! We cannot let them take it down without a fight."

With a plan in mind, Anne grabbed her clipboard and pen. "We need to gather signatures from the community to show how much everyone values that tree. Luna, you can help us spread the word!"

Luna's eyes sparkled with excitement. "I'll do my best!" she replied, feeling a surge of determination.

They set off together, with Luna leading the way. They visited the park, where families were enjoying picnics, children were playing, and everyone loved the old oak tree. Luna approached people, meowing gently to get their attention, while Anne explained the situation.

"Would you like to help us save this beautiful tree?" Anne asked, holding out the clipboard for signatures. The response was overwhelmingly positive. "Of course! That tree is our favourite spot!"

With each signature they gathered, Luna felt more hopeful. Apollo, meanwhile, entertained the children with his playful antics, ensuring everyone was in high spirits while they worked.

As they continued their campaign, they also spoke to local businesses and community members, sharing stories about the tree's importance and its role in the neighbourhood. Luna even suggested organizing a "Save the Tree" event, where people could come together to celebrate it with music, food, and fun activities.

By the end of the day, they had gathered a significant number of signatures and made a lot of noise about their cause. Luna felt proud of their efforts. "I think we might actually save it!" she said, her heart swelling with hope.

Anne smiled, looking at the impressive stack of signatures. "With this support, we can present our case at the next council meeting. Together, we will make sure the tree is saved!"

That evening, as they returned to Anne's office, Luna felt a deep sense of accomplishment. Not only had she rallied her friends and community, but she had also grown closer to Anne and Apollo in the process.

"I'm so glad we did this together," Luna said, purring contentedly. "Thank you for believing in me and the tree!"

"Always," Anne replied, giving Luna a gentle scratch behind the ears.

As Luna settled down in a cozy corner of the office, she thought about her favourite oak tree and all the adventures that lay ahead. She knew they would do everything they could to protect it, and she felt grateful to have such wonderful friends by her side. Together, they were a force to be reckoned with, ready to stand up for what they loved.

10

Luna was filled with excitement as she prepared for her playdate with her little friend, Oscar. Oscar was a spirited young boy with an imagination as colourful as his smile, and Luna always loved the adventures they shared together.

Pete helped Luna into her favourite colourful collar, and soon they were on their way to Oscar's house. The familiar route was filled with lovely sights: blooming flowers, friendly neighbours, and the gentle rustle of leaves in the breeze. Luna could hardly contain her excitement as they arrived.

Oscar greeted them at the door, his face lighting up with joy. "Luna! You came!" he exclaimed, bending down to give her a gentle hug. Luna purred happily, nuzzling his hand. "Are you ready for some fun?" Oscar asked, his eyes sparkling. "I have a new game we can play!"

Luna followed Oscar inside, her tail flicking with curiosity. The living room was filled with toys, and in the corner stood a colourful tent that Oscar had set up. "It's a fort!" Oscar said proudly. "We can pretend we're on a treasure hunt!" "Oh, that sounds amazing!" Luna meowed, imagining all the adventures they could have.

They crawled into the fort together, and Oscar brought out a treasure map he had drawn. "We have to find the hidden treasures in the house!" he said, pointing to various spots marked with colourful crayons.

Luna felt a thrill of excitement. "Let's go, Captain Oscar!" she meowed puffing out her chest as if she were a brave adventurer.

Their first stop was the kitchen, where Oscar looked high and low for the "golden cookie." Luna helped by sniffing around, her whiskers twitching with determination. After a few moments, Oscar spotted a cookie jar on a shelf. "There it is!" he shouted, jumping with joy.

With a little boost from Pete, they got the jar down, and Luna got a small piece of cookie as a reward. "Yum!" she purred, savouring the sweet treat.

Next, they ventured into the living room, searching for more treasures. Oscar pointed to the bookshelf, and Luna hopped up to inspect the colourful books. As she nudged one with her paw, a small shiny toy fell out from behind. "We found it!" Oscar cheered, clapping his hands in delight. "Two treasures down, one to go!" Luna exclaimed, feeling like a true treasure hunter. Their last stop was the garden. Oscar and Luna dashed outside, where Oscar's imagination transformed the flowers into mystical islands. "The final treasure is hidden among the flowers!" he announced, his eyes scanning the colourful blooms.

Luna sniffed around, her nose twitching with excitement. After a moment, she spotted a small sparkly ball buried near the rose bushes. "I see it!" she called out, pawing at the ball until it rolled out into the open. "We did it!" Oscar shouted, picking up the ball and holding it high. "We're the best treasure hunters ever!"

As they sat down on the grass, Luna felt warm and happy. She loved spending time with Oscar, sharing laughter and adventures. They played with the shiny ball, tossing it back and forth, enjoying the warm sun on their faces.

As the afternoon ended, Oscar hugged Luna tightly. "Thank you for the best playdate ever! I cannot wait for our next adventure!" Luna purred, snuggling into his embrace. "Me too, Oscar! You make every day special."

With hearts full of joy, they headed back inside.

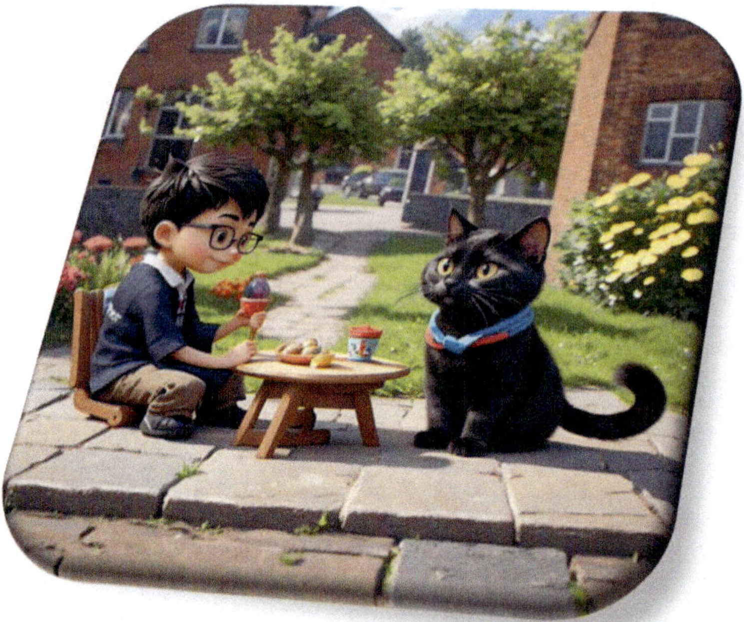

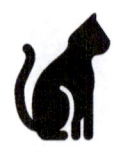

11

Luna was enjoying a leisurely stroll through town when she spotted her friend Peter, the local photographer, looking a bit lost. He was standing in front of a map, scratching his head. Curious, Luna trotted over to him. "Hey, Peter! What is going on?" she meowed, tilting her head. "Oh, hey, Luna!" Peter replied with a sigh. "I am trying to find the perfect coffee shop. I have heard so much about them, but I just cannot seem to locate one that feels right."

Luna's ears perked up. "I can help with that! I love exploring, and I know all the best spots in town!" "Really? That would be amazing!" Peter said, his eyes lighting up. Together, they set off on their little adventure, Luna leading the way with her tail held high. "There are a few popular spots I can think of. Let us start with Brewed Awakenings, they have the most delicious pastries!"

As they walked through the bustling streets, Luna pointed out different landmarks and shops, sharing little titbits along the way. "And if you are looking for something unique, there is a place called Cat's Whiskers Café. They have a cat themed menu, and sometimes they even have adoptable cats!"

Peter chuckled. "That sounds adorable! I would love to check that out."

When they arrived at Brewed Awakenings, the warm scent of freshly brewed coffee wafted through the air. Luna nudged the door open with her paw, and they stepped inside. The café was filled with comfy chairs, soft music, and friendly staff.

"See? It is so inviting!" Luna meowed, hopping up onto a nearby chair to take in the atmosphere.

Peter smiled as he walked up to the counter. "I'll have a latte, please!" he said to the cheerful woman behind the counter, who was pouring a steaming cup of coffee. While he waited, he glanced around and admired the cozy decor.

After a few moments, the woman handed Peter his drink, and they found a spot by the window. Luna settled comfortably on the chair next to him, her eyes gleaming with excitement. "So, what do you think?"

"It is perfect! But I feel like I should keep exploring. What else do you recommend?" Pete replied, taking a sip of his latte.

Luna thought for a moment. "Next, we should try the Cat's Whiskers Café. It is just a short walk away, and you will love their cat-themed drinks!"

They made their way to Cat's Whiskers Café, and as they approached, Luna noticed a sign that read "Adoptable Cats Inside!" She felt a wave of happiness wash over her, knowing that more furry friends could find their forever homes. Inside the café, the walls were adorned with cat art, and the menu featured whimsically named drinks like "Purrfect Brew" and "Meowcha." Luna watched as customers played with the adorable cats lounging around.

Peter ordered a "Purrfect Brew" and found a cozy spot again by the window where he could sip his coffee and watch the antics of the adoptable cats. "This place is amazing, Luna! I can see why you love it so much."

"I knew you'd enjoy it!" Luna purred, her tail flicking with delight. "It's all about the joy of being surrounded by friendly faces, both human and feline."

As they sat together, enjoying their drinks and the lively atmosphere, Luna felt a sense of fulfilment. Helping Peter find the perfect coffee shop had turned into a delightful afternoon filled with laughter, warmth, and a bit of feline charm.

After finishing their drinks, Peter looked at Luna with a big smile. "Thanks for your help, I think I have found not one, but two perfect coffee shops!"

Luna purred happily, feeling proud of their little adventure. "Anytime. There are always more places to explore together."

With that, they left the café, both looking forward to their next adventure

12

Luna decided to explore the nearby duck pond. She padded quietly through the tall grass and her ears perked up, listening for the soft quacking of the ducks. As she approached the pond, she spotted a lively group of ducks waddling about, splashing in the water, and chasing one another playfully.

Among them was a particularly bold duck named Daphne. With her colourful feathers and curious nature, she was known to be the life and soul of the pond. Daphne was always eager to make new friends, and today, she was just about to have an unexpected visitor.

Luna cautiously stepped closer, her heart racing with excitement. The ducks noticed her and paused their antics, with curiosity. "Who's that?" quacked one of the smaller ducks. Daphne- always the brave one- waddled up to Luna. "Hello there! I am Daphne. Are you here to join the fun?" Her voice was cheerful, and Luna felt a warmth in her heart.

"I'm Luna," she purred softly, "I just moved here. I've never seen a duck pond before."

Daphne's eyes sparkled with delight. "Well, you're in for a treat! We have races, splash contests, and even some excellent diving tricks. Want to join us?"

Luna paused for a moment and then meowed: "I'd love to!", her tail flicking with excitement.

The ducks gathered around as Daphne explained the rules of their race. "We will line up at the edge of the pond, and when I say 'Go!' we will all jump in and swim to the other side. Ready?"

Luna nodded. The ducks lined up, and with a loud quack, Daphne shouted, "Go!" They all leaped into the water, splashing, and flapping their wings. Luna, feeling a rush of excitement jumped up and down on the bank, watching, amazed by their graceful movements.

After several rounds of racing, Luna decided to try something daring. "Can I dive in too?" she called out.

The ducks cheered her on. "Of course! Just be careful!" Daphne encouraged.

Taking a deep breath, Luna gathered her courage and jumped in, landing with a splash. The cool water enveloped her, and she paddled with all her might, laughing as she tried to keep up with her new friends. The ducks quacked with joy, and soon they were all swimming together, splashing and playing in the afternoon sun.

As the sun began to set, Luna, and Daphne floated side by side, tired but happy. "You're a great swimmer for a cat!" Daphne exclaimed.

Luna smiled: "Thank you, Daphne. I have had so much fun."

From that day on, every afternoon, Luna would visit the pond, and together they would create new adventures, explore the world around them, and share stories.

13

One bright morning, Luna woke up with a craving for her favourite treats- the ones with a crunchy, fish-flavoured centre that had mysteriously vanished from her food bowl. Determined to satisfy her craving, she decided to go on a little adventure around the neighbourhood.

As she slipped out of her cozy home, the world outside seemed full of possibilities. The sun was shining, and the air was filled with the sweet scent of blooming flowers. Luna's keen nose twitched with excitement. "Just a quick search," she thought, "and I'll be back in no time!"

With her heart set on treats, she pranced through the garden and out into the street. She padded past blooming hedges and friendly neighbours, her eyes wide with wonder. However, the search quickly turned into an adventure. Luna followed the scent of fish that wafted from a nearby open window. It led her further and further from home.

Before she knew it, Luna found herself in the town's bustling market, the air thick with enticing aromas. Stalls overflowed with fresh produce, and stall holders shouted out their wares. The sight was overwhelming, and Luna, caught up in the excitement, wandered deeper into the crowd.

After a while, she realized she had strayed far from home. The treats she sought were nowhere in sight. Panic began to set in as she looked around, her heart racing. The market seemed vast and unfamiliar, and the voices of people and sounds of busy life blurred into one.

Just as Luna felt a wave of despair wash over her, she spotted a friendly face. It was a young girl named Petra, who often visited the pond with her family. "Luna! What are you doing here?" she exclaimed, bending down to stroke Luna's soft fur.

"I was looking for treats," Luna meowed, barely above a whisper. "But now I can't find my way home."

Petra's eyes softened with understanding. "Don't worry. I will help you!" She gently picked up Luna and cradled her in her arms. "Let's find you some treats first, and then I'll take you home."

With that, they ventured to a nearby pet shop. Inside, Luna's eyes widened at the sight of shelves lined with all sorts of delicious goodies. Petra selected a small bag of fish-flavoured treats, and Luna could hardly contain her excitement.

Once outside, Petra opened the bag, and Luna savoured her first treat, blissfully crunching it as they made their way back to her home. With every step, Luna felt her worries fade away. She was still a little lost, but with Petra by her side, she felt safe.

After a short walk filled with laughter and chat, they arrived back at Luna's house. Petra set her down gently. "Here you are, safe and sound! I am glad we found those treats," she said with a smile.

Luna purred gratefully; her belly now full of fishy goodness. She rubbed against Petra's legs, thankful for her kindness and help. "You're the best!" she meowed.

As Petra waved goodbye and headed home, Luna settled back into her cozy spot, her heart warm from the adventure and the friendship. From that day on, Luna learnt to always keep track of her surroundings.

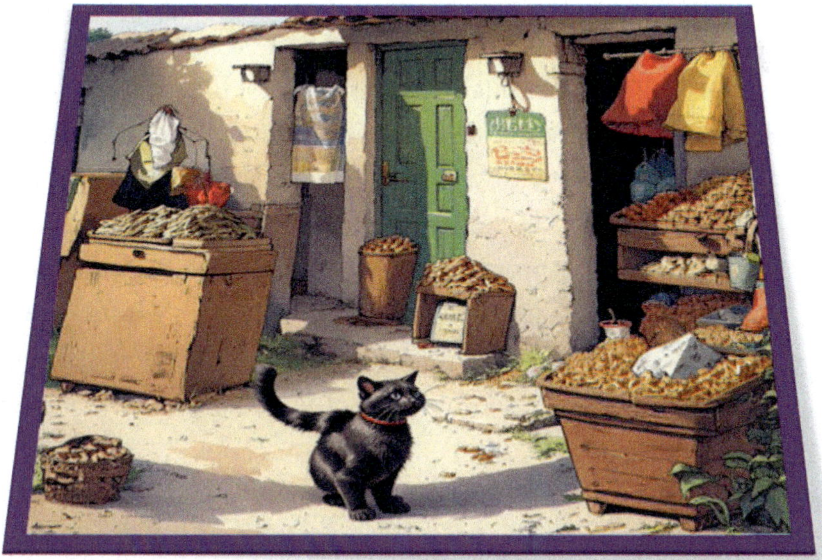

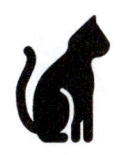

14

Having explored most of her neighbourhood, Luna decided it was time she visited the train station, a place she had heard so much about from the other animals in the area. Rumour had it that Bernie, the station master, always had a few treats tucked away for his furry friends. With her tail held high and excitement bubbling inside her, Luna made her way through the winding streets until she reached the bustling train station. The sound of trains whistling, and the chatter of travellers, filled the air. Luna's eyes sparkled with curiosity as she observed the comings and goings of passengers.

As she trotted along the platform, she spotted Bernie, a kind-hearted man with a bushy beard and a warm smile. He was checking tickets and greeting passengers as they boarded the train. Luna watched him for a moment, her whiskers twitching with anticipation.

"Excuse me, Mr. Bernie!" she meowed out- a meow so soft that it caught his attention.

Bernie knelt, his eyes twinkling. "Well, if it isn't Luna! What brings you here today?"

"I heard you have the best treats in town!" she purred, rubbing against his leg. "Can I have some please?"

Chuckling, Bernie reached into his pocket and pulled out a small bag of cat treats. "You heard right! I always keep a few for my favourite feline visitors." He offered her a treat, and Luna eagerly accepted it, savouring the delicious chicken flavour.

After her snack, Luna wanted to explore more of the station. Bernie noticed her adventurous spirit. "Want a little tour, Luna? There is plenty to see!"

Luna's eyes widened with delight. "Oh, yes, please!"

Together, they wandered around the station. Bernie showed her the old clock that had been ticking for decades, the ticket booth with its colourful posters, and even the cozy waiting room filled with travellers reading books and sipping coffee. Luna loved the way the sunlight streamed through the windows, casting warm patches on the floor where she could bask.

As they walked, they stumbled upon a little girl sitting alone, looking worried. Luna's instincts kicked in. She gently approached the girl, who had lost her teddy bear during the hustle and bustle of the station.

"Don't worry!" Luna meowed softly, nuzzling the girl's hand. "We can help you find it."

With Bernie's guidance, they searched high and low under benches, behind suitcases, and near the ticket counter. Finally, just as the girl was about to lose hope, Luna spotted a familiar plush shape peeking out from behind a trash can.

"There it is!" she exclaimed, bounding over to retrieve the teddy bear. With a proud flick of her tail, she presented it to the girl, who squealed with delight.

"Oh, thank you! You are the best cat ever!" the girl cried, hugging Luna tightly.

Bernie smiled, watching the heartwarming scene. "You've got quite the knack for helping others, Luna."

After a few more rounds of exploration, Bernie led her back to the platform, where he had prepared a small farewell treat for her.

"Thanks for visiting, Luna. You're always welcome here," he said, giving her a gentle scratch behind the ears.

With a satisfied purr and a heart full of joy, Luna knew she had found a special place in the train station and a wonderful friend in Bernie.

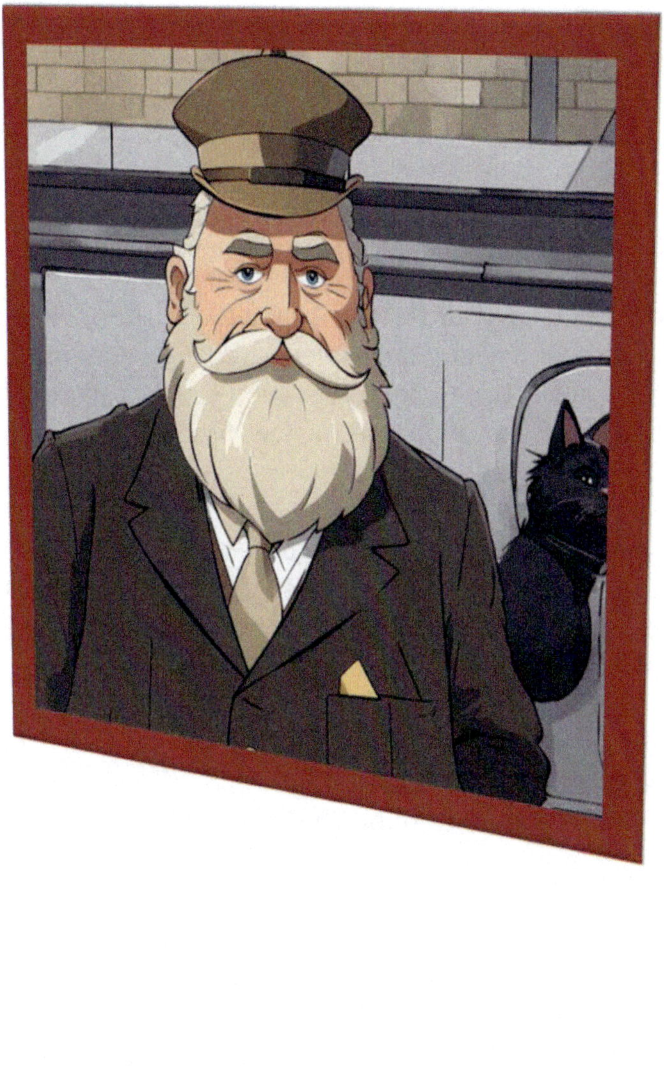

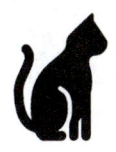

15

Luna stood on a wall in the market square watching the streets of her little town that were bustling with activity - children played, dogs were barking, and neighbours chatted, but Luna's keen eyes soon caught sight of Mandy, the sweet lady who lived a few houses down from her human mum and dad.

Mandy was standing on the corner, looking around with a puzzled expression. Luna sensed that she was trying to find her way home, but with all the new road signs and building work going on, it was clear she was a bit lost.

Concerned for her friend, Luna jumped down from her perch and trotted over to her. Mandy, looked down and smiled as she spotted the little black cat.

"Oh, Luna! What a lovely surprise!" Mandy said, kneeling to give her a gentle scratch behind the ears. "I'm afraid I've gotten a little bit lost, can you help me find my way home? "Luna nodded; her heart filled with determination. She had always loved helping others, and this was her chance to assist someone she cared about. With a flick of her tail, she led the way down the street, her paws quick and confident.

As they walked, Mandy chatted about her day, telling Luna about the flowers she wanted to plant in her garden and the delicious pie she had baked that morning. Luna listened intently, occasionally glancing back to ensure Mandy was following her.

They turned left at the park, where children were playing on swings and laughing. Luna paused for a moment, watching them with wide eyes, then continued. Mandy chuckled. "I remember when I used to play there! Time flies, doesn't it?"

After a few more turns, they found themselves at the corner of Maple Street. Mandy's face lit up with recognition. "Oh! I know this place! My house is just a little further down."

Luna's heart swelled with joy. She quickened her pace, leading Mandy down the familiar path. Finally, they reached her cozy cottage, with its bright flowerbeds and cheerful red door.

Mandy bent down and hugged Luna tightly. "Thank you so much, dear! I do not know what I would have done without you. You are a true friend!"

Luna purred happily, feeling the warmth of Mandy's affection. "Just doing my job!" she meowed.

Before heading inside, Mandy opened her door and called back to Luna. "Come by later! I have made a fresh apple pie, and I would love to share a slice with you!"

Luna's eyes sparkled at the thought. "I'll be there!" she meowed; her heart warm with happiness as she trotted back home. Luna felt a warm glow of satisfaction.

16

While Luna was lounging, bathed in her favourite sunbeam in the garden, she heard an excited voice coming from close by. It was Susie, her human mum- a lovely young woman with a passion for storytelling and a talent for broadcasting her own radio show. Luna had always admired Susie's creativity, and she decided to join her.

As Luna approached, she noticed the door was slightly ajar. Curious, she pushed it open with her paw and padded inside. The living room was filled with colourful posters, a microphone set up on a table, and sound equipment scattered about. Susie was busy adjusting the dials on her radio equipment, her brow furrowed in concentration.

"Hi, Luna!" Susie exclaimed, her face lighting up when she saw her furry friend. "I'm just getting ready for my next show, but I could really use some help!"

Luna tilted her head, intrigued. "What do you need help with?" she purred.

"I'm planning to do a special segment about animals in our town," Susie explained. "But I need someone to help me with sound effects and a few stories! Do you think you could assist?" Luna's eyes sparkled with excitement. "Absolutely! I would love to help!"

Together, they got to work. Susie began by setting up the microphone, while Luna listened intently as Susie shared her ideas. They decided to include sounds that represented the town's animals like the cheerful chirping of birds, the soft rustling of leaves, and the occasional barking of dogs.

Luna took her role seriously. She scampered around the room, trying to mimic the sounds they needed. For the chirping birds, she created a soft trill by purring lightly, while for the rustling leaves, she gently swished her tail against the table. Susie laughed, delighted by Luna's creativity. "That's perfect! You are a natural at this!"

As they worked together, Susie shared fun facts about the animals in their town. Luna contributed stories of her own adventures- like the time she helped Mandy find her way home or when she explored the train station with Bernie. Susie recorded everything; her eyes wide with enthusiasm.

After an hour of laughter and creativity, they had gathered a treasure trove of stories and sound effects. Susie beamed with pride. "This is going to be the best show ever!"

As the time for the broadcast approached, they prepared to go live. Susie adjusted the microphone and took a deep breath. "Welcome to the Animal Adventures Show!" she announced excitedly. "Today, we're featuring a special guest: Luna the Cat!"

Luna perked up, feeling a rush of excitement as Susie began the show. They shared the stories they had created together, along with Luna's carefully crafted sound effects. The mix of laughter and animal sounds filled the air, creating a delightful atmosphere.

As the broadcast continued, Luna felt a sense of joy. She had not only helped Susie create something special, but had also strengthened their friendship through creativity and collaboration.

When the show came to an end, Susie beamed with satisfaction. "Thank you so much, Luna! You were amazing!"

Luna purred happily, her tail flicking with pride. "I had so much fun! Let us do it again sometime!"

As Susie signed off and celebrated their successful broadcast, Luna basked in the warm glow of friendship, knowing that their teamwork had created something truly special. With the sun setting outside, she looked forward to more adventures both on the radio and beyond.

17

One Sunday morning, Luna was hiding in her favourite patch of long grass when she spotted her friend David, a young artist known for his love of urban sketching and alleyways. He was looking a bit lost, standing at the edge of the park with a sketchbook in hand and a furrowed brow.

Curious, Luna trotted over. "Hey, David! What is going on?" she meowed. David sighed, glancing at his sketchbook. "I am trying to find some interesting alleyways to draw, but I cannot remember where the good ones are. I want to capture the hidden beauty of the city!" Luna's ears perked up at the challenge. "I can help you with that! I know all the nooks and crannies around here. Let us go explore!" David's face brightened. "Really? That would be awesome!"

Together, they set off into the heart of the city. Luna led the way, her sleek black form darting through the bustling streets. They turned down a narrow street lined with colourful murals, each telling a story of the neighbourhood.

"This way!" Luna said, leading David toward a small alleyway adorned with hanging plants and fairy lights. "This is one of my favourites. It is full of character!"

David pulled out his sketchbook and began to draw. As he sketched, Luna sat beside him, soaking up the sun and keeping an eye on the world around them. She loved the way David captured the alley, his pencil dancing across the page.

"Wow, this is amazing!" he said, glancing at his work. "I never would have found this place without you."

Luna purred with pride. "There are more hidden spots nearby! Let us keep going."

They ventured deeper into the town, discovering more alleyways. One led them to a cozy café with outdoor seating, another to a small courtyard with a fountain surrounded by colourful flowers. Each spot inspired David, who filled his sketchbook with colourful drawings.

"Let's try that alleyway over there!" Luna suggested, pointing with her paw to a narrow passageway that looked intriguing. As they entered, they found themselves in a hidden market filled with treasures and handmade crafts.

David's eyes widened with excitement. "This place is fantastic! I cannot believe I did not know it was here."

Luna watched as he quickly set up to draw a stall filled with handmade pottery.

The colours were rich and inviting, and she admired how David captured the spirt of the market in his sketches.

As the day went on, Luna and David explored countless alleyways, each one revealing a unique charm. They chatted and laughed, sharing stories and ideas. With every new discovery, David's sketches came to life, brimming with the energy of the town.

Finally, as the sun began to set, David painted the sky with hues of pink and orange, and they found a quiet spot to rest. David looked through his sketches, a satisfied smile on his face. "Thank you so much, Luna. I could not have done this without you. You have a real gift for finding the hidden gems in the town!"

Luna purred, curling up beside him. "I love helping my friends discover new places. This was so much fun!"

Their adventure through the alleyways had turned into a memorable day filled with creativity and friendship.

"Let's do this again sometime," he said, looking down at Luna. "You're the best guide I could ask for."

With a contented purr, Luna agreed, already dreaming of their next adventure through the town's hidden corners.

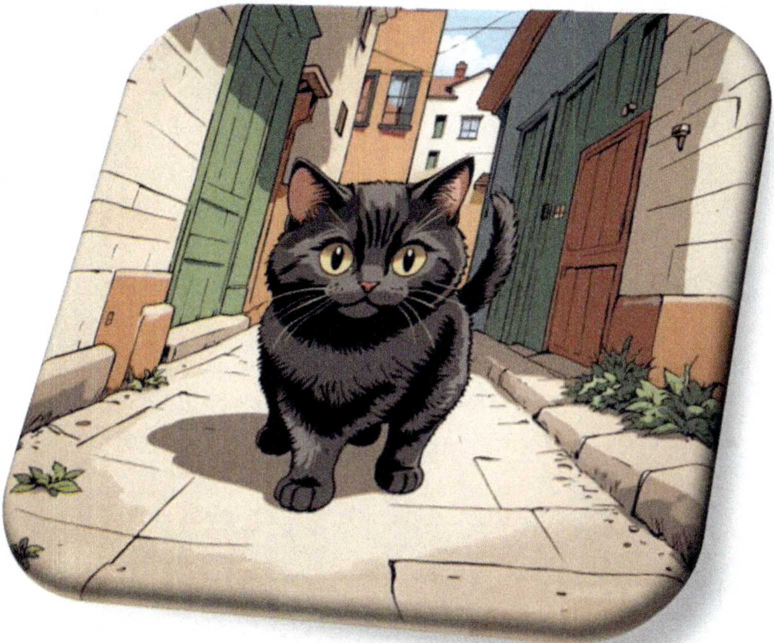

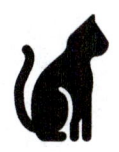

18

Luna decided it was time for an adventure beyond her familiar neighbourhood. She had heard stories from other animals about the bustling town and all the exciting things to see. With her heart full of curiosity, she set off toward the bus stop.

As she arrived, she spotted a familiar face behind the wheel of the bus. Robert was a cheerful bus driver known for his kind heart, and he often shared little treats with her whenever they met.

"Good morning, Luna!" Robert called, waving as he opened the bus door. "Are you ready for a ride into town?"

Luna hopped up the steps, her green eyes sparkling with excitement. "Yes, please! I cannot wait to see what is there!"

As the bus pulled away from the stop, Luna settled in a cozy window seat. She watched the scenery change from quiet streets to bustling sidewalks filled with people, shops, and colourful signs. The town was alive with energy, and Luna's heart raced with excitement.

"First stop, the market!" Robert announced over the intercom. "They got fresh produce, baked goods, and all sorts of goodies."

Luna's ears perked up at the mention of food. She loved the scent of fresh bread and pastries! When the bus came to a halt, she could not wait to hop off.

The market was a feast for the senses. Stalls overflowed with colourful fruits, fragrant herbs, and delicious baked goods. Luna explored, weaving between shoppers' legs, her nose twitching as she took in all the delightful smells.

"Luna!" Robert called, catching up with her. "Do you want to help me pick out some treats for the bus? I will let you choose!"

Luna's eyes widened with delight. "Really? That sounds perfect!"

Together, they strolled through the market. Luna selected a few tasty snacks; some fresh fish for herself and a couple of pastries for Robert. As they gathered their goodies, Robert chatted with the stall holders, sharing stories and laughter.

After their shopping spree, they headed back to the bus, and Robert prepared to continue their journey. "Next stop, the park! There is a lovely fountain and plenty of space to play." Luna purred with excitement, and as the bus rolled toward the park, she gazed out the window, watching families enjoying picnics and children playing games. When they arrived, she hopped off eagerly.

The park was stunning. Tall trees swayed in the gentle breeze, and the sound of laughter filled the air. Luna ran to the fountain, where the water sparkled in the sunlight. She dipped her paw into the cool water, splashing playfully.

"Looks like you're having fun!" Robert laughed, leaning against the fountain. "I'll keep an eye on our treats while you explore."

Luna played for a while, chasing butterflies, and exploring the flowerbeds. She met other animals in the park- a friendly dog, a curious squirrel, and even a couple of birds. They all joined in her playful antics, making her adventure even more delightful.

After a bit of playtime, Luna returned to Robert, who had set up a little picnic by the fountain. They shared the pastries, and Luna savoured the fresh fish, feeling content and happy.

"Thank you for today, Robert!" Luna said, her eyes shining. "This has been such a great adventure!"

Robert smiled warmly. "Anytime, Luna! You're always welcome on my bus. Let us head back home when you are ready."

The ride back was filled with stories and laughter, and as they approached home, Luna felt grateful for her friend Robert and the wonderful day they had shared.

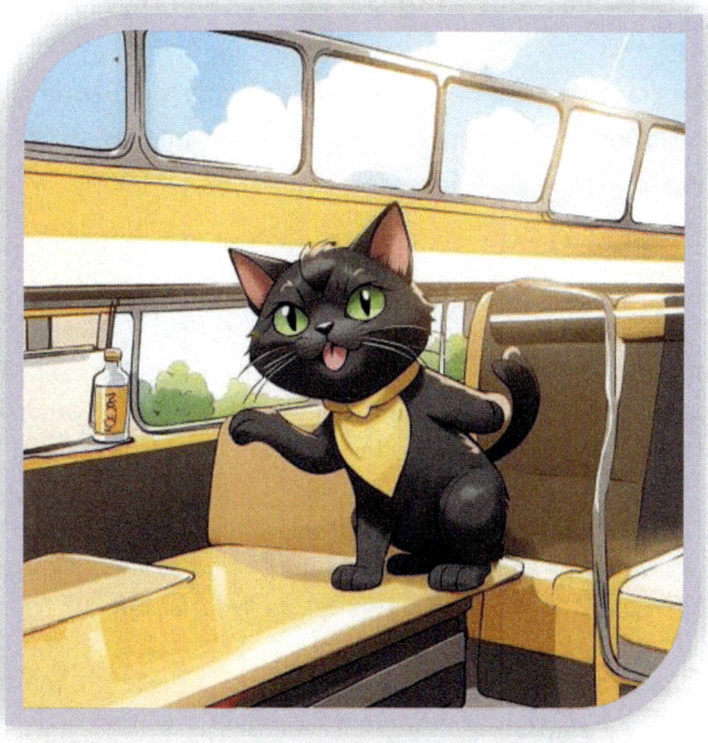

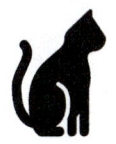

19

Luna noticed something unusual. The dust bin- a familiar fixture in her cozy home- was missing! Luna loved exploring the contents of the bin especially the crumpled paper and the occasional forgotten treat wrapper.

Curious and a bit concerned, Luna jumped down and trotted through the house, searching for clues. She peeked under the kitchen table, but no sign of the dust bin. She padded into the living room, checking behind the couch, but it was still nowhere to be found.

Just then, her human family member Susie walked in. "Oh, Luna! Have you seen the dust bin? I had to take it outside to empty it, but I cannot remember where I put it!"

Luna's ears perked up. "Outside? That is where the mystery lies!" she thought, her adventurous spirit ignited.

Susie smiled, noticing Luna's inquisitive gaze. "I guess we should go look for it together!"

They headed outside, where the warm sun cast playful shadows on the ground. Luna and Susie searched the garden first. They checked near the flower beds and around the patio, but the dust bin was still missing.

"Maybe it rolled away," Susie suggested, looking down the path that led to the alley. "Let's check there!"

With a determined leap, Luna dashed ahead, her little paws padding softly on the pavement. As they turned the corner, they found themselves in the alley, which was lined with colourful murals and the scent of blooming plants. Luna's nose twitched with excitement.

Suddenly, she spotted a familiar shape tucked behind a stack of crates. "There it is!" she meowed, racing over. Sure enough, it was the dust bin, but it looked a bit different- someone had covered it in colourful stickers!

Susie chuckled as she approached. "Looks like the neighbourhood kids got creative! I had no idea they could turn my old dust bin into a work of art."

Just then, a group of children appeared, giggling. One of them, a little girl called Anne Whitehead, waved. "Hey! That is our project! We borrowed it to use for our art." Susie laughed, a twinkle in her eye. "You have done a wonderful job! I hope it is okay to bring it back home now."

Anne nodded, beaming with pride. "Of course! We were just finished. Do you want to keep the stickers on it?"

Luna's tail flicked with excitement. The idea of having a decorated dust bin was thrilling! Susie thought for a moment. "I think that would be fun! It will make cleaning up a little more special."

With the dust bin now a colourful piece of art, Susie and Luna carefully rolled it back home, the stickers catching the sunlight and sparkling as they walked.

Once back inside, Susie placed the dust bin in its usual spot, now transformed into a unique decoration. Luna purred with delight, feeling proud of their little adventure.

From that day on, Luna not only enjoyed exploring the dust bin but also admired the creativity of her neighbours.

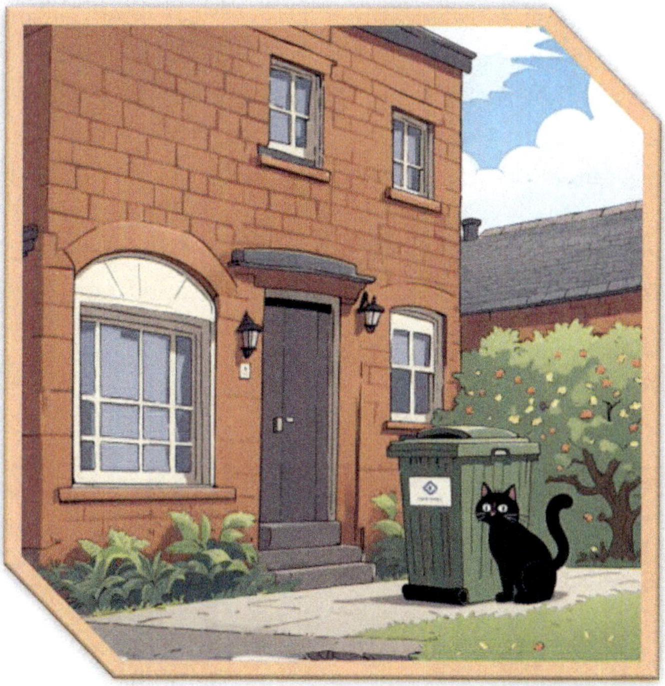

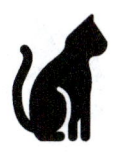

20

One night, Luna felt a curious urge to explore the old graveyard on the edge of her town. She had heard whispers of it from the other animals; stories filled with mystery and intrigue. Tonight, the full moon bathed the graveyard in a silvery glow, and Luna's adventurous spirit could not resist.

As she padded quietly through the wrought iron gates, Luna felt a shiver of excitement. The tall gravestones loomed like silent guardians, and the soft rustle of leaves added to the eerie atmosphere. "Just a little exploration," she thought, her heart racing with both fear and thrill.

As she wandered deeper into the graveyard, she noticed something unusual- a faint, shimmering light drifting among the stones. Luna's curiosity piqued. "What could that be?" she wondered, creeping closer.

Suddenly, the light flickered and took on a ghostly shape, revealing a figure that appeared to be a young woman in a flowing dress. Luna's fur bristled, but she could not help but feel intrigued rather than scared.

"Hello, little cat," the ghostly figure said softly, her voice gentle and melodic. "I am Mari, the guardian of this graveyard. I have been watching over it for many years."

Luna tilted her head, her fear melting away. "A guardian? What do you guard?" she asked, her green eyes wide with curiosity.

"I protect the memories of those who rest here," Mari replied, gliding gracefully among the stones. "But lately, some of the spirits have been restless. They need help to share their stories and find peace."

Luna's heart swelled with empathy. "How can I help?" she asked, her adventurous spirit ignited.

"Would you help me listen to their stories?" Mari asked. "Many of them have unfinished tales. If you could share their stories with the living, it would bring them comfort."

Luna nodded eagerly. "I'd love to!"

Mari led Luna to different gravestones, where each spirit had a unique story to tell. One spirit was a brave soldier who longed to be remembered for his courage. Another was a kind baker who wanted everyone to know how much joy she found in sharing her treats.

As Luna listened attentively, she felt a warmth in her heart. Each story was filled with love, laughter, and a touch of sadness, but they all carried an important message. With every tale, she felt more connected to the past.

After they had gathered the stories, Luna turned to Mari "What should we do now?"

"Tomorrow, you can share these stories with the townspeople," Mari suggested. "Hold a gathering at the park, and let everyone know about the lives of people who lived here. It will help the spirits find peace."

Luna was excited by the idea. "I will tell them all! They deserve to be remembered!"

With a soft smile, Mari floated closer. "Thank you, dear Luna. You are braver than you know."

As the moon began to sink, Mari faded into the night, leaving Luna with a sense of purpose. The next day, she shared the stories with the townspeople, inviting everyone to gather in the park. As she recounted each tale, the community listened with rapt attention, feeling the connection to those who had come before them.

When Luna had finished, the townspeople felt a sense of warmth and understanding. They decided to create a memorial in the park, honouring the lives of those in the graveyard, ensuring that their stories would never be forgotten.

From that day on, the graveyard felt different. The spirits, now at peace, watched over the town with gratitude. And Luna, the little black cat who had listened to their stories, knew she had made a difference in the lives of many both living and departed.

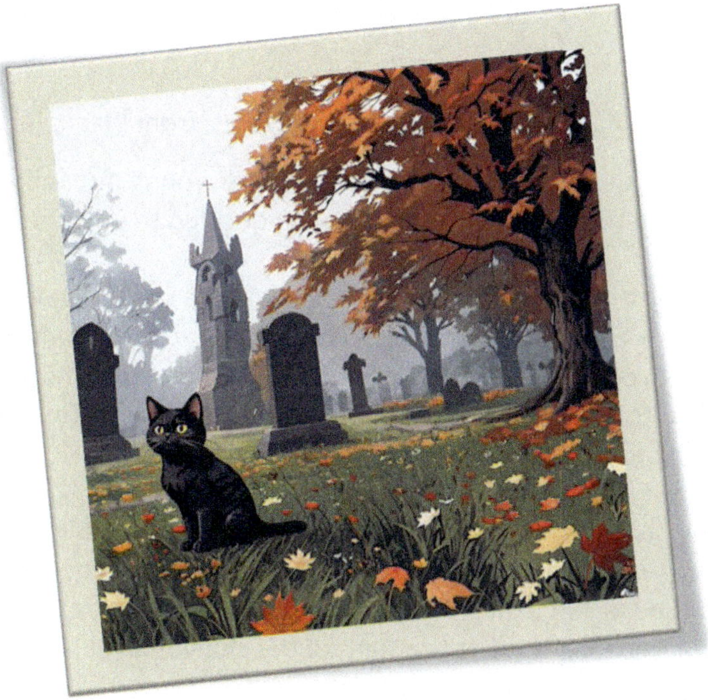

21

Luna had heard fascinating tales from her friends about the nearby fire college, where young firefighters trained to be heroes. Intrigued, she decided to pay a visit.

As she approached the college, Luna could see the building was bustling with activity. Students in bright uniforms practiced drills, and the sound of laughter and shouting filled the air. Luna's eyes widened in excitement. This was going to be an adventure!

She slipped through the open gate and wandered into the courtyard. There, she spotted a group of students gathered around a large fire truck, discussing their next exercise. Luna's heart raced at the sight of the shiny red vehicle.

"Hey, look at that cute cat!" one of the students exclaimed. "Is she here to join the team?"

Luna paused, tilting her head as if considering the offer. "Why not?" she thought. "I could learn a thing or two about being brave!"

Just then, a kind voice called out. "Welcome to the fire college! I am Nigel, one of the instructors. Would you like to join us for a demonstration?"

Luna purred happily, feeling welcomed. "I would love to!" she purred

Nigel led Luna and the group to a training area where they practiced using hoses and rescue techniques. The students showed off their skills, spraying water and climbing ladders. Luna watched with wide eyes, fascinated by their teamwork and dedication.

"Want to see something cool?" Nigel asked, as he knelt to Luna's level. He proceeded to demonstrate how to connect a hose to the fire truck. "This is how we get water to fight fires. But it takes practice and teamwork!"

Luna nodded, feeling inspired. "Teamwork is important!" she thought.

After the demonstration, the students took a break. They shared stories about their experiences, and Luna listened intently, soaking in their tales of bravery and friendship. Each story was filled with lessons about helping others and facing fears.

One student, Lilly, noticed Luna's interest. "You know, Luna, being a firefighter is not just about fighting fires. It is about being a friend and helping the community."

Luna purred in agreement, her tail flicking with enthusiasm. "That sounds just like what I love to do!"

After their break, Nigel proposed a fun challenge. "How about we set up an obstacle course? Let us see how quickly you can navigate through it!"

Luna's ears perked up at the idea. "An obstacle course? I am in!" she meowed ready to showcase her agility.

The students set up a course with cones, tunnels, and small jumps. Luna dashed through it, her movements graceful and swift. The students cheered her on, and she felt like a true champion.

"Great job, Luna!" Lilly called out as Luna finished the course. "You'd make a great firefighter!"

Luna beamed with pride. She may have been only a small cat, but today she felt like a hero.

As the sun began to set, casting a warm glow over the college, Nigel gathered everyone together. "Thank you, Luna, for joining us today. You have shown us that bravery comes in all sizes!"

Luna purred, feeling a sense of belonging. She had learned so much and made new friends at the fire college. With a grateful heart, she waved goodbye to her new friends, promising to return for more adventures.

As she trotted home, Luna felt inspired by her day at the fire college. She realized that being brave and helpful did not require a uniform; it was about caring for others and being part of a community. With that thought in mind, she looked forward to sharing her newfound wisdom with her friends.

22

Luna noticed her human friend Daphne pacing around the living room with a worried look on her face. Luna tilted her head, curious about what was troubling her.

"Luna!" Daphne sighed, looking down at her furry friend. "I need a new pair of shoes, but I cannot find anything I like! My old ones are falling apart."

Luna's ears perked up at the mention of an adventure. "A shopping trip? I am in!". After all, a trip to the shoe store meant new experiences and maybe even some fun along the way.

Daphne grabbed her bag and called, "Let's go, Luna!" She opened the door, and together they set off toward the nearby shopping district.

As they walked, Luna could sense Daphne's frustration. She wanted to help. "Maybe I can help you find the perfect shoes!" she meowed, her little tail flicking with determination.

Once they arrived at the shoe shop, Luna hopped out of the bag and began exploring. The bright lights and colourful displays filled the shop with energy. Daphne began browsing the shelves, trying on different pairs. Each time she slipped on a new shoe, Luna would jump up to inspect it closely.

"These ones feel too tight," Daphne said, discarding a pair. "And these are too boring."

Luna thought for a moment. She remembered how Daphne loved bright colours and stylish designs. She darted towards a colourful display in the corner, where a pair of stunning red trainers caught her eye. With a playful paw, she nudged them forward.

"Luna, what did you find?" Daphne asked, coming over. Her eyes widened as she saw the shoes. "Wow! These are bold!"

Luna purred with approval, happy to have made a good suggestion. Daphne picked up the red trainers, examining them closely. "They are cute! I will try them on."

As Daphne slipped on the shoes, Luna watched intently. They fitted perfectly! Daphne beamed as she looked in the mirror. "I love them!" she exclaimed. "They're fun and comfortable!"

Luna felt a sense of accomplishment. "I knew you'd like them!" she meowed, purring with pride.

"Let's get these!" Daphne decided, heading to the checkout. "Thanks for your help, Luna. You have a great eye for style!"

After paying for the shoes, they stepped back outside. The sun was shining, and the air was filled with excitement. "Now, let's take a walk to show off my new trainers!" Daphne said, grinning.

As they strolled through the park, Daphne admired her new shoes with each step. Luna walked proudly beside her, enjoying the fresh air.

"Shopping for shoes can be so hard," Daphne said, giving Luna an affectionate scratch behind her ears. "But today was fun because you were with me."

Luna purred, knowing she had helped her human friend find something special. Together, they enjoyed the rest of their day, exploring the park and basking in the warm sunshine - a perfect ending to their little adventure.

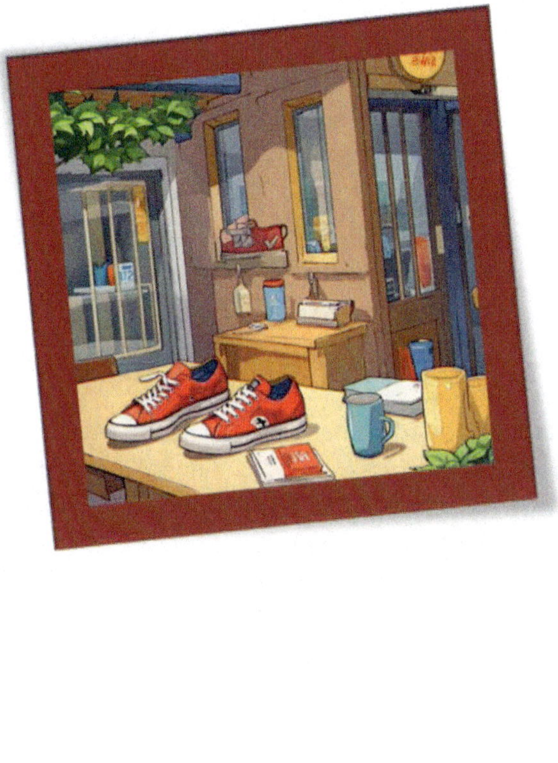

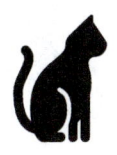

23

On hearing a loud commotion coming from the next room, Luna padded quietly along the wooden floor to investigate.

When she entered the room, she found her Susie in a bit of a pickle. The table was covered in colourful craft supplies, but what caught Luna's attention was the thick, sticky glue that seemed to be everywhere!

"Oh no, Luna! I have made such a mess!" Susie exclaimed, looking around. Glue dripped from the table, and her hands were covered in it, too. "I was trying to make a beautiful collage, but I think I got a little carried away!"

Luna tilted her head, "I can help!" she meowed. First, Luna jumped onto the table, carefully navigating the sticky chaos. "Let's start by cleaning up a bit," she purred, trying to be encouraging. "Maybe we can find a way to fix this together!"

Susie nodded, taking a deep breath. "Okay! But how do I even begin?"

Luna hopped down to the floor and motioned for Susie to follow. "Let us gather some paper towels and a bowl of warm soapy water. That should help with the glue!"

With renewed determination, Susie collected the supplies while Luna supervised, making sure everything was in order. They tackled the mess together - Susie wiping down surfaces while Luna playfully swatted at stray bits of glue that had dripped to the floor.

As they worked, Luna could not help but pounce on the glistening droplets of glue, making Susie giggle. "You're such a silly kitty!" Susie laughed, as they continued cleaning.

After they cleared up most of the glue, Susie looked at her half-finished collage, which was still in a bit of a mess. "I don't know if I can save this," she sighed.

Luna thought for a moment, then had an idea. "Why not turn this into a new project? We can create something even more fun!"

Susie's eyes lit up. "You are right! I can use the colourful paper and make a new collage! Let's do it!"

With Luna by her side, Susie gathered fresh materials. They cut out shapes, arranged colours, and even added a few bits of glitter. Luna helped by nudging papers into place with her paws and playfully batting at the glitter, sending sparkles into the air.

As they worked together, the room filled with laughter and creativity. Susie felt inspired, and Luna's playful spirit kept the energy high. By the time they had finished, they had transformed the original mess into a stunning, vibrant collage that reflected their teamwork and friendship.

"Look at what we created!" Susie exclaimed, holding it up proudly. "It's even better than before!"

Luna purred in agreement, thrilled to have helped turn a sticky situation into a masterpiece. As they admired their work, Susie gently scratched behind Luna's ears. "Thank you for being such a great helper, Luna. I could not have done this without you!"

As they cleaned up the last bits of glue and glitter, Luna felt happy with the fun they had shared and excited for their next creative project together.

24

One autumn day, Luna decided it was the perfect time to visit her friend Amanda, the town historian. Amanda was known for her knowledge of the town's history and her fascinating stories about the past. Luna loved hearing her tales, and today, she felt especially curious about the old landmarks around town.

As Luna padded through the charming streets, she admired the colourful leaves swirling in the breeze. Soon, she arrived at Amanda's little house, filled with books, maps, and all sorts of historical treasures. Luna hopped up onto the porch, her tail flicking with excitement.

"Hello, Luna!" Amanda greeted, opening the door with a warm smile. "I was just organizing my collection of old photographs. Would you like to help?"

Luna purred in agreement, stepping inside. The cozy room smelled of aged paper and ink, and the walls were lined with shelves filled with books and artifacts. Amanda spread out a large map of the town on the table, and Luna jumped up to take a closer look.

"What do you want to learn about today?" Amanda asked, glancing at Luna. "There are so many interesting stories!"

Luna's eyes sparkled as she pointed a paw at the old clock tower marked on the map. "What about this one? I have seen it in the town square, but I want to know more!"

Amanda's face lit up. "Ah, the clock tower! It has a rich history. It was built over a century ago and was once the tallest structure in town. It served as a meeting point for the community and has witnessed many important events."

Luna listened intently as Amanda shared tales of town gatherings, celebrations, and even a few mishaps that had happened around the clock tower. "One winter, the town held a festival to celebrate the first snowfall, and everyone gathered at the tower to watch the snowflakes dance in the air," Amanda recounted, her eyes sparkling with nostalgia.

"That sounds magical!" Luna exclaimed, her imagination running wild.

Encouraged by Luna's enthusiasm, Amanda pulled out an old photograph of the clock tower surrounded by townsfolk, laughing, and celebrating. "This was taken during that very festival! You can see how happy everyone was."

Luna leaned in closer, captivated by the smiles and the festive atmosphere in the photo. "I wish I could have been there!"

"Who knows, Luna?" Amanda said with a smile. "Maybe we can recreate some of that joy today! How about we plan a little gathering around the clock tower next week? We can invite friends to share stories and celebrate our town's history."

Luna's eyes widened in excitement. "That would be wonderful! We could even bring treats!"

"Yes!" Amanda agreed, her voice bright with enthusiasm. "Let's make it a day to remember, just like the festivals of the past."

The two friends spent the afternoon planning the event, making lists of who to invite and what snacks to bring. Luna suggested some local treats she had seen in the bakery, and Amanda wrote everything down, her heart full of joy at the thought of bringing the community together.

As the sun began to set, Luna and Amanda admired the map once more. "There's so much history in this town," Luna said, feeling a sense of connection to the stories of those who came before her.

"Indeed, there is," Amanda replied, a thoughtful look in her eyes. "And it is important to keep those stories alive. You have helped inspire something beautiful today, Luna."

With a warm purr, Luna felt proud to have played a part in celebrating their town's history. As she said her goodbyes and headed home, she looked forward to the gathering, eager to create new memories while honouring the old.

In the days to come, Luna would not only share her love for the clock tower but also weave herself into the fabric of her town's story, one gathering at a time.

25

Being at home for the day Luna decided it was a perfect day for a visit to her friends Rosco, Bob, and Blinky. The three cats lived in a cozy house at the end of the street, with Amanda, the town historian and Ben her husband. Luna always loved spending time with them- they had all sorts of adventures together.

As she padded her way down the path, Luna thought about what fun they might have. Rosco was known for his clever tricks, Bob had a knack for finding the best sunspots, and Blinky was always full of imaginative ideas. When she arrived at their home, she was greeted by the familiar sounds of purring and playful meowing.

"Luna!" they all called out in unison, their eyes lighting up with excitement.

"Hello, everyone!" Luna replied, her tail flicking happily. "What are we up to today?"

Rosco, a sleek ginger with a mischievous glint in his eye, jumped down from the window sill. "We were just talking about how to catch the biggest butterfly in the garden! Want to join us?"

Blinky, a fluffy tabby cat with big expressive eyes, bounced excitedly. "Yes! But first, we need a plan. Butterflies are tricky!"

Bob, a laid-back grey cat lounging in a sunny spot, nodded. "Let us gather some supplies. Maybe we can create a little butterfly-catching kit!"

With that, the four friends headed to Bob's favourite sunny corner, where they found bits of string, a small net, and some colourful ribbons. Luna's eyes sparkled with excitement as they brainstormed ways to catch butterflies without harming them.

"Let's make a colourful trap to attract them!" suggested Blinky. "Butterflies love bright colours!"

With Luna leading the way, they worked together to create a butterfly-catching contraption. They hung ribbons from branches and arranged the net beneath them, making it look like a beautiful little garden.

Once everything was set up, they waited patiently, their eyes scanning the garden for any fluttering visitors. Time passed, and just as they were about to give up, a lovely butterfly appeared, dancing through the air. It was vibrant and graceful, with wings that sparkled in the sunlight.

"There it is!" Rosco whispered, excitement bubbling in his voice. "Get ready!"

As the butterfly fluttered closer, Luna felt her heart race. They all held their breath, hoping their plan would work. The butterfly landed on one of the colourful ribbons, and in that moment, Luna and her friends sprang into action!

With a gentle swoop, they tried to catch the butterfly in the net. But just as quickly as they moved, the butterfly took flight, swirling around them in a playful dance. Luna giggled; her eyes wide with delight. "It's too fast!"

"Maybe we should just watch it instead," Bob suggested, stretching out lazily. "It's beautiful to see it up close."

Blinky nodded, realizing the joy in simply observing the butterfly's graceful movements. "You are right! Let us enjoy the moment."

They all settled down, watching the butterfly as it flitted from flower to flower, its colours shimmering in the afternoon light. Luna felt a warm glow of happiness as she sat with her friends, sharing in the beauty of nature.

"Sometimes it's better to appreciate things rather than try to catch them," Luna purred thoughtfully.

Rosco smiled. "And we did have fun making our butterfly trap together!"

As the sun began to set, painting the sky in shades of orange and pink, the four friends knew they had created a wonderful memory - one filled with laughter, teamwork, and the beauty of friendship.

With happy hearts, they headed inside, excited to share their butterfly adventure with everyone. Luna felt grateful for her friends and the delightful day they had spent together, knowing that their bond was as beautiful as the butterflies they had chased.

26

One sunny Sunday morning, Luna decided to explore the bustling car boot sale happening in the town square. The air was filled with the sounds of chatter, laughter, and the occasional clinking of coins. Luna loved the colourful surroundings and the chance to see all sorts of interesting items and meet new friends.

As she wandered through the rows of cars and tables, Luna noticed a familiar face -Theresa, the local artist, was setting up her stall. Luna had always admired Theresa's colourful paintings and whimsical sculptures. With a flick of her tail, she made her way over to greet her.

"Luna!" Theresa exclaimed, her eyes lighting up. "What a lovely surprise! Are you here to shop for something special?"

Luna purred, "I am just exploring! I love seeing all the treasures people bring to the car boot."

Theresa smiled and gestured to her stall. "I have brought some of my smaller paintings and a few art supplies. I thought I could inspire others to create their own art!"

Luna's eyes sparkled as she looked at the colourful paintings. Each one was a delightful splash of colour, showing scenes of nature, cats, and whimsical landscapes. "They are beautiful, Theresa! You always have such a way with colours."

"Thank you, Luna!" Theresa replied, her cheeks flushing with pride. "I am trying to encourage people to find their creative side. Would you like to help me? We could set up a little art corner for kids and families to try painting!"

Luna's ears perked up at the idea. "That sounds like so much fun! Let us do it!"

Together, they gathered some supplies- small canvases, brushes, and a rainbow of paints. They set up a cozy corner near Theresa's stall, complete with a colourful banner that read "Art Corner: Unleash Your Creativity!"

As the day went on, families began to gather around, intrigued by the invitation to create. Children's laughter filled the air as they painted, splattering colours, and letting their imaginations run wild. Luna sat nearby, watching with delight as the kids giggled and chatted while they worked.

One little girl, her face smudged with paint, looked at Luna and asked, "Can cats be artists too?"

"Of course!" Luna meowed with a playful flick of her tail. "Art is for everyone, whether you have paws or hands!"

Theresa laughed and added, "Exactly! Just like Luna, you can express yourself in any way you like."

The art corner quickly became a hit, with children and adults alike creating their own masterpieces. Luna even got a few paint splatters on her paws as she playfully explored the area, bringing smiles to everyone around.

As the sun began to set, casting a golden glow over the square, Luna looked around at the colourful canvases drying in the light. Each painting was unique, filled with joy and creativity. "This has been the best day!" she meowed; her heart full.

Theresa, her face beaming, replied: "It truly has! Thank you for helping me make this happen. You have brought so much joy to everyone here."

Luna purred happily, feeling proud of their little art corner. "I just love seeing everyone express themselves. It is wonderful to create together!"

As the car boot sale began to wind down, Luna and Theresa shared stories and laughter, feeling grateful for the memories they had created that day. They knew they had not only brought art to life but also fostered a sense of community and connection among their friends and neighbours.

With the evening air growing cooler, Luna waved goodbye to Theresa and the new friends they had made. As she trotted home, she could not help but think about how art, like friendship, was a beautiful way to bring everyone together.

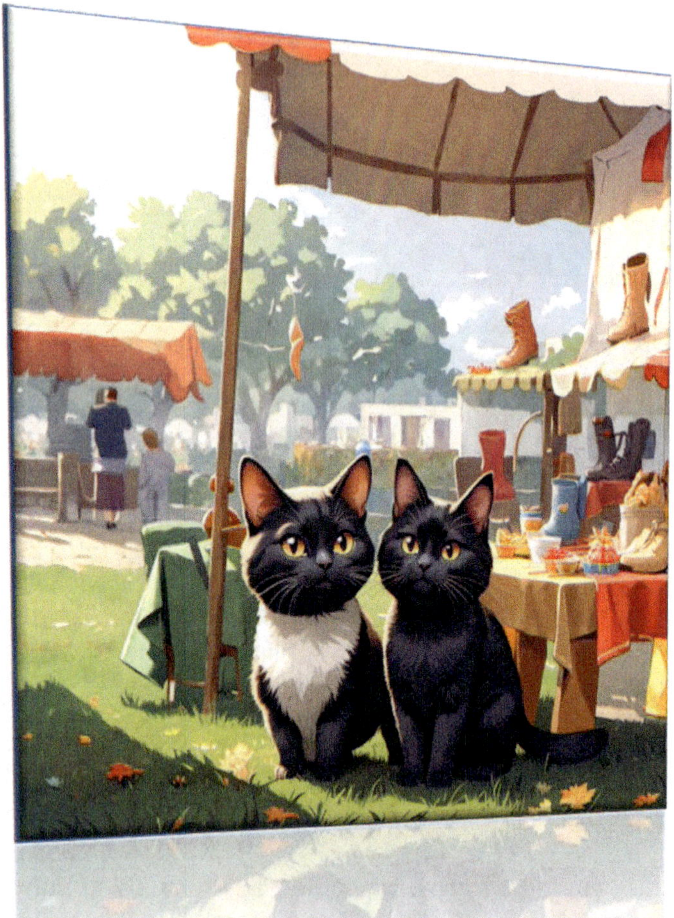

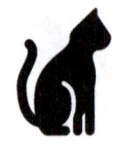

27

Luna was buzzing with excitement. She had heard that a concert featuring her favourite local musicians - Massimo, Laura, Anna, and Kate - was happening in the park. The thought of live music filled her with joy, and she could not wait to experience it for the first time.

As she padded through the park, Luna could already hear the faint sounds of instruments tuning and people chatting. Colourful lights twinkled in the trees, and a crowd was gathering near the stage. Luna's heart raced with excitement.

When she arrived, she spotted Massimo-a talented keyboardist known for his soulful melodies- setting up his equipment. "Hey, Luna!" he called out, waving. "Are you ready for a night of music?"

"I can't wait!" Luna meowed, her tail flicking with excitement. She loved how music brought everyone together, and she was thrilled to be part of it.

As the sun began to set, the stage lights came on, illuminating the area in a warm glow. Laura and Anna, known for their enchanting harmonies, took to the stage next, their voices intertwining beautifully. Luna found a cozy spot on a blanket laid out near the front, feeling the vibrations of the music flowing in her little paws.

As the concert continued, Massimo took to the stage, his powerful voice filling the park. The crowd erupted in cheers, and Luna could not help but sway to the rhythm. The energy was contagious, and she felt completely immersed in the moment.

Then it was Kate's turn. She was known for her upbeat songs that always got everyone dancing. As she strummed her guitar and sang, Luna could not resist the urge to tap her paws along with the beat. The crowd clapped and sang along, creating an atmosphere of pure joy.

With each song, Luna watched the musicians connect with their audience, sharing stories and laughter between performances. She felt inspired by the way they brought everyone together through their art.

As the night went on, Massimo invited the audience to join in on a sing-along. Luna, feeling bold, leaped onto the stage. The crowd gasped in surprise, then erupted in laughter and applause as she began to meow along to the music, her little body swaying side to side.

"Look at Luna go!" Laura exclaimed, joining in with her guitar. The audience cheered, and Luna felt like a star in her own right. It was a magical moment; one she would cherish forever.

After the concert, the musicians came down to greet their fans. "You were fantastic up there, Luna!" Kate said, giving her a gentle pat. "You've got real stage presence!"

Luna purred, feeling proud and happy. "Thank you! I had so much fun!"

As the night ended and the crowd began to disperse, Luna felt a sense of community and connection that filled her heart with warmth. She had not only enjoyed the music but had also created memories that would last a lifetime.

With a joyful flick of her tail, Luna made her way home, her mind still swirling with melodies. She could not wait to tell her friends about her first concert experience, where she had danced and sung alongside her favourite musicians under the stars. It had been a night to remember, and she looked forward to many more adventures filled with music and friendship.

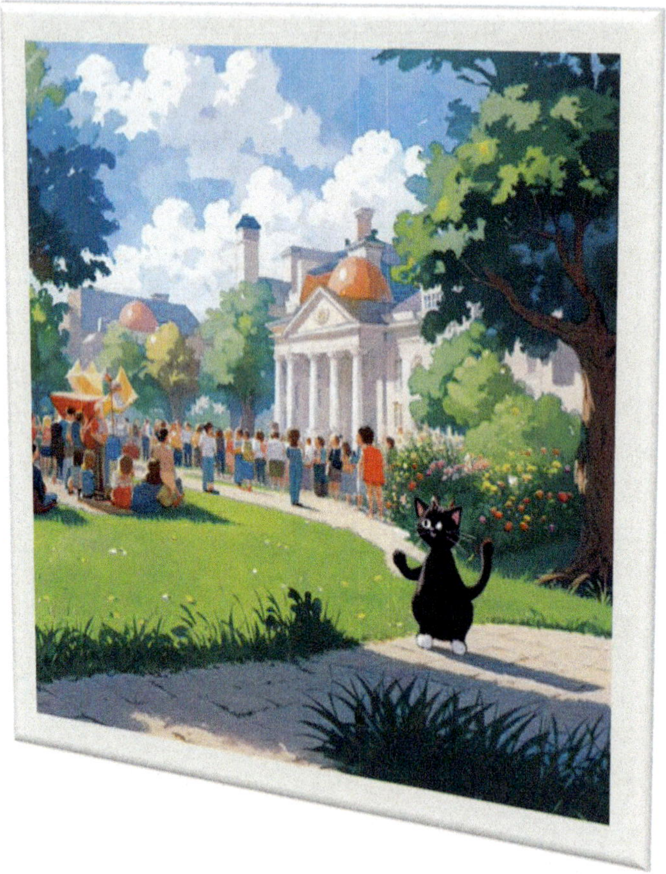

28

One eerie evening, Luna the cat was prowling in her garden. The air was filled with the scent of autumn leaves and something... strange. Her whiskers twitched in curiosity as she ventured further, feeling a mix of excitement and caution. Suddenly, a rustling noise came from the bushes, followed by a low groan. Luna's fur stood on end, and she crouched low, ready to bolt if needed. Out of the shadows emerged a figure, stumbling and dragging its feet- not a usual nighttime visitor. It was a zombie!

Luna's first instinct was to flee, but something about the zombie intrigued her. It had a tattered shirt and a puzzled expression, as if it were just as confused as she was. Instead of attacking, it looked around, moaning softly.

"Uh... are you lost?" Luna called out, her voice steady despite her surprise. The zombie turned its head slowly, eyes wide with surprise. "Grrr... I am... looking for... brains?" it said in a raspy voice- but it did not sound menacing, more like it was searching for something familiar.

Luna, realizing this zombie did not seem dangerous, decided to approach. "Well, you might have come to the wrong neighbourhood for that! But I can help you find something else to eat if you would like."

The zombie blinked, momentarily forgetting its original quest. "Food? I... I like food!"

With a playful flick of her tail, Luna led the way to one of her favourite spots in the garden, where a few leftover treats from earlier were scattered about. "Here, try some of these! Much tastier than brains!" The zombie hesitated, then knelt, sniffing the treats. "Mmm... smells good!" It took a hesitant nibble, and its eyes lit up with delight. "This is... amazing! "Luna purred, pleased to see the zombie enjoying itself. "See? There is more to life than just brains!"

As they shared the snacks, Luna learned that the zombie, named Ben, had once been a regular guy before a mishap turned him into a zombie. "I just want to fit in again," Ben confessed, his eyes looking a little less vacant.

Luna thought for a moment and said, "Why not try joining in on Halloween festivities? People dress up as zombies! You could be a hit!" Ben's face lit up. "Really? I would love that!

As Halloween approached, Luna and Ben became an unlikely duo, planning their big night. When the time came, Ben was a hit! Kids laughed and cheered, enjoying the friendly zombie who gave out treats instead of scaring them away. From that night on, Luna and Ben became great friends, proving that even the most unexpected encounters can lead to delightful friendships and adventures.

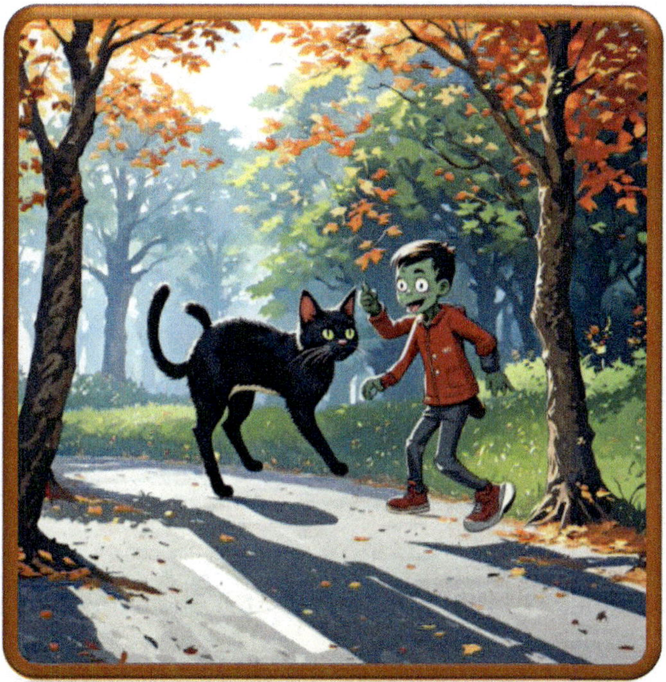

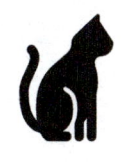

29

Waking to the sound of birds chirping, a gentle breeze and the rustling of leaves outside- feeling adventurous, Luna decided to visit the pond. With a flick of her tail, she set off.

When Luna arrived at the pond, she was captivated by the sparkling water and the gentle ripples. The sun danced on the surface, creating a mesmerizing effect. As she approached the edge, she noticed some fish darting about beneath the surface, their scales glinting in the sunlight.

Luna sat quietly, watching them swim, her mind buzzing with thoughts. "I wonder if I could catch one," she mused, remembering the stories of cats who were expert fishers. After a moment of thought, she decided to give it a try. She crouched low, her eyes focused on the water. With a graceful leap, she swiped at the surface, but the fish were too quick and darted away. "Okay, okay," she thought, regaining her composure. "I'll be stealthier this time."

Taking a deep breath, Luna focused on her surroundings, tuning into the rhythm of the pond. She moved slowly, inching closer to the water's edge. Just then, she spotted a plump fish that had wandered too close by. With a determined flick of her paw, she struck again.

This time, Luna was successful! She managed to hook the fish with her paw, but as it flopped around, she realized she had not quite thought this through. The fish splashed and wriggled, and Luna found herself slipping on the wet grass. With a surprised yowl, she tumbled into the shallow water!

Spluttering and soaked, Luna emerged from the pond, shaking off the droplets. The fish, meanwhile, had flopped back into the water, looking none the worse for wear. Luna could not help but laugh at herself, the cool water refreshing her.

"Okay, maybe fishing isn't my strong suit," she chuckled, glancing around. Just then, she spotted a friendly turtle sunbathing on a nearby rock. "Hey, you!" Luna called. "Do you have any tips for catching fish?"

Terry the turtle poked her head out, looking amused. "Well, you have got the enthusiasm down! But patience is key. Try waiting for the fish to come to you instead of chasing them."

Taking Terry's advice, Luna settled down by the pond's edge, watching the water intently. She stayed still and quiet, letting the sounds of nature wash over her.

After a while, a few curious fish began to swim closer, drawn by her calm presence. With newfound patience, Luna waited until just the right moment, then quickly swiped at the water again. This time, she was ready! She caught a little fish in her paws, holding it up triumphantly. "Look! I did it!" she exclaimed, grinning at the turtle. The turtle clapped her flippers together in encouragement. "Well done! But remember, fishing is also about enjoying the moment."

With a satisfied purr, Luna decided to release the fish back into the pond, letting it swim away freely. She realized that the fun was not just in catching but in the adventure itself.

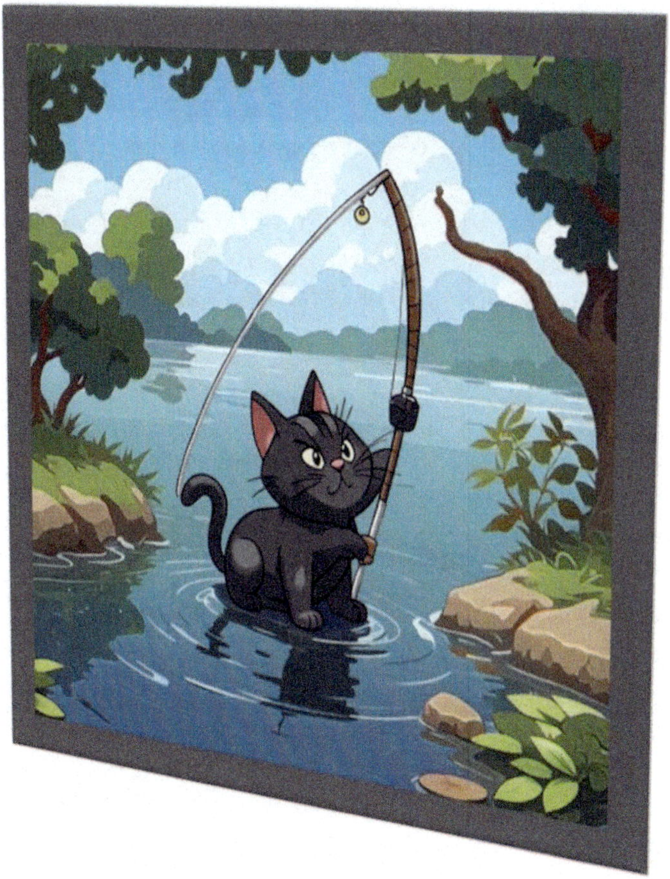

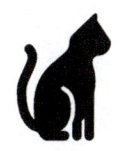

30

One spring morning as Luna stretched and yawned, she noticed a flurry of movement in the bushes nearby.

Curious, Luna tiptoed over to investigate. To her surprise, she discovered a fluffy white figure with long ears hopping about- it was the Easter bunny! The bunny was busy hiding colourful eggs amongst the flowers, but it seemed to be in quite a rush.

"Need some help?" Luna meowed out, tilting her head. The bunny paused, looking startled but relieved. "Oh, hello! Yes, please! I am the Easter Bunny, you can call me Grace, and I have got so many eggs to hide before the children come out to find them. I could use a little extra paws-on help!"

Luna's eyes sparkled with excitement. "I would love to help! Where do you need me?" With a grateful nod, the Easter Bunny explained the plan. "We need to spread these eggs all around the garden. I will take care of the higher spots, and you can hide them in the flower beds and bushes."

They quickly got to work, Luna darted between colourful flowers, carefully placing the eggs in clever spots. She found a perfect spot among the tulips and another nestled in a patch of daisies.

As they worked, the bunny shared stories about the magic of Easter and the joy of seeing children's faces light up when they discovered the hidden eggs. Luna was fascinated, her heart was warming to the thought of spreading happiness.

After a while, they took a break, enjoying the sunshine and the lovely spring day. "You know," the bunny said, munching on a carrot, "I have always thought cats were quite clever. You have a real knack for this!"

Luna purred, flattered by the compliment. "Thanks! I never knew hiding eggs could be so much fun. It feels good to help!" Just as they were finishing up, they heard the distant sound of laughter. The children were coming! "Quick, we need to hide!" the Easter Bunny said, hopping behind a bush. Luna quickly found a cozy spot in the crook of a tree, her tail flicking with excitement. As the children raced into the garden, their eyes lit up with joy at the colourful eggs scattered around.

The Easter Bunny watched with delight, and Luna felt a rush of happiness, knowing she had played a part in creating this joyful moment.

Once the children had gathered all the eggs, Luna and the bunny emerged from their hiding spots, both grinning from ear to ear. "Thank you, Luna! You were a wonderful helper!" the bunny said, giving her a little nudge with her nose. "I had fun!" Luna purred, feeling proud of their teamwork.

As the day ended, the Easter Bunny waved goodbye, promising to come back next year. Luna settled back in her sunny spot, her heart full of joy, knowing that she had not only made new memories but also a new friend. And from that day on, every spring would remind her of the magical Easter adventure she shared with Grace.

31

Luna was curled up on the windowsill, watching raindrops race down the glass. The soothing sound of the rain made her drowsy, and she was about to nod off when she heard a faint scurrying sound coming from the pantry.

Curious, Luna hopped down and padded quietly toward the source of the noise. As she peeked inside, she spotted a small grey mouse, its tiny nose twitching as it rummaged through a bag of treats that had been left open.

Luna's instincts kicked in, and she crouched down low, ready to pounce. But as she watched the little mouse, something stopped her. The mouse looked up, startled, and met Luna's gaze. Instead of fear, there was a hint of defiance in those tiny eyes.

"Hello! I am just trying to get a snack!" the mouse squeaked, puffing out its chest. "It is not my fault your human left the food out! "Luna blinked in surprise. She had never talked to a mouse before. "You shouldn't be in here," she replied, her tone more curious than threatening. "You could get into a lot of trouble!"

The mouse paused, its whiskers twitching. "Yes, well, I am hungry, and it is raining out there! I need to eat!"

Luna thought for a moment. She remembered her own favourite treats and how nice it felt to share with friends. "What if I help you? There are some crumbs on the floor in the dining room. It is safer than rummaging through the pantry," she suggested.

The mouse looked sceptical but intrigued. "You'd really do that?"

"Why not?" Luna meowed with a playful flick of her tail. "I am not going to eat you. I just want to make sure you stay safe."

With a cautious nod, the mouse agreed. Luna led the way to the dining room, where they found a few crumbs left from the last meal. As they shared the snack, they began to chat, discovering they had more in common than they thought.

"I'm George, by the way," the mouse said between nibbles.

"I'm Luna," she replied, feeling a warm sense of a new friendship.

As the rain continued to pour outside, Luna and George spent the afternoon exchanging stories. Luna told tales of her adventures around the house and town, while George shared his stories off running around inside walls and under the floorboards.

Eventually, the rain slowed to a drizzle. George looked up at Luna, a twinkle in his eye.

"Thanks for being so nice. Most cats would chase me away."

"Maybe not all cats are as scary as you think," Luna replied with a playful grin.

As the sun began to peek through the clouds, George decided it was time to head back home. "I will see you around, Luna. Maybe we can have another snack together sometime?"

"I'd like that," Luna said, watching him scamper away with a newfound friendship in her heart.

From that day on, Luna and George continued their unlikely friendship.

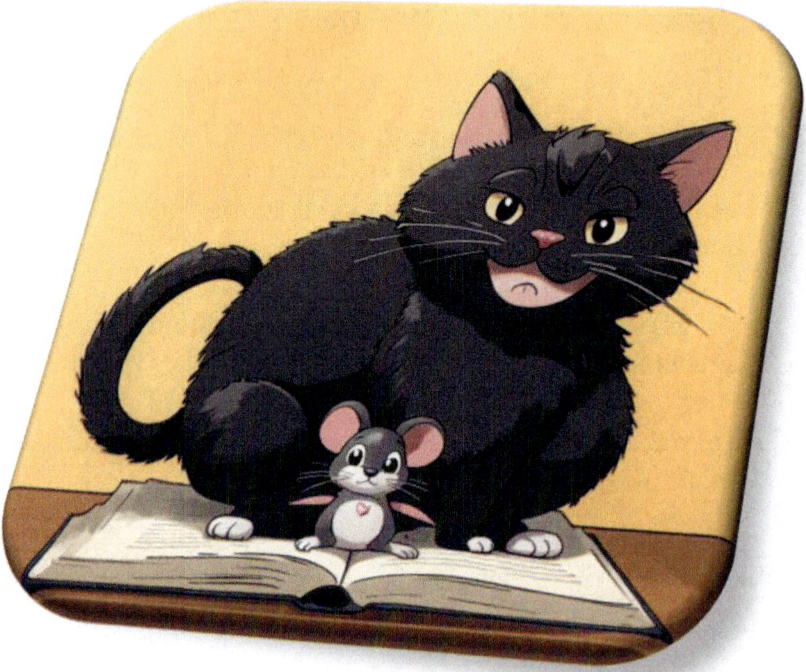

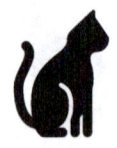

32

Luna lifted her head as she heard a faint, sad meowing coming from the nearby bushes. Her ears perked up, and her curiosity was piqued. Without a second thought, she jumped to her feet and trotted over to investigate.

As she got closer, the meowing grew louder, and Luna's heart sank. She pushed aside some branches and discovered a tiny grey kitten, tangled in some twigs and looking scared. The little one was shivering, unable to free itself.

"Hang on, little one," Luna meowed gently, trying to reassure the kitten. The kitten looked up with wide, frightened eyes, his tiny body trembling. Luna carefully pawed at the twigs, her movements gentle and precise. After a few moments of careful work, she managed to free the kitten from its entrapment.

The little kitten blinked up at Luna, seemingly in awe. "Thank you!" he squeaked, his voice still trembling. Luna felt a swell of pride. "No need to thank me! But you really should be more careful," she said, her tone light and playful.

With the kitten now free, Luna led the way back to her house, making sure to keep an eye on her new friend. As they reached the garden, Luna showed the kitten around, pointing out the best sunny spots and the safest hiding places.

The kitten began to relax, starting to pounce playfully after leaves and shadows. Luna watched with amusement; her heart was warming at the sight of the little one finding joy again. "What's your name?" she asked.

"Dexter" the kitten meowed, looking a bit lost. "I got separated from my mum."

Luna's heart ached for the little one. "Well, let's find her together," she suggested. They spent the afternoon searching the neighbourhood, Luna guiding the kitten with gentle nudges and encouraging purrs.

As the sun began to set, they heard a familiar meow in the distance. Luna perked up her ears. "Do you hear that?" she asked excitedly. The kitten's eyes lit up, and they both hurried towards the sound.

Soon, they found a worried mother cat pacing near a bush. The moment she spotted her kitten, she rushed over, nuzzling him with relief. "Oh, my dear! I was so worried!" she meowed, tears of joy in her eyes.

Luna watched, her heart swelling with happiness at the reunion. The kitten looked up at Luna and said, "Thank you for rescuing me. You are the best!"

With a gentle purr, Luna replied, "Just doing what friends do." She waved goodbye as the mother and kitten headed off together, grateful for their reunion.

33

Early one Monday morning Luna woke up to the sound of children laughing and chatting as they headed off to school. Feeling curious and wondering what all the excitement was about, she decided to follow them.

As she trotted along, Luna found herself at the school's entrance, staring at the kids with her wide, green eyes.

They were bustling around, backpacks slung over their shoulders, books in hand. Feeling bold, Luna slipped through the open door and into the hall.

Inside, the classrooms were filled with colourful posters and the sounds of learning. Luna continued to pad quietly down the hallway, her soft paws barely making a sound. Suddenly, she peeked into a classroom and saw a teacher explaining something on the board, while students took notes. Intrigued, she decided to join in.

The children gasped when they spotted her. "Look! A cat!" one exclaimed. The teacher smiled and said, "It looks like we have a special visitor today!" Luna took this as an invitation and leapt gracefully onto the teacher's desk, where she settled comfortably.

The students giggled and began asking questions. "What's her name?" "Can she do tricks?" "Does she like tuna?" Luna purred contentedly, enjoying the attention. The teacher decided to use Luna to teach about animals, discussing their behaviour and habitats.

After a fun lesson, the bell rang, signalling break time. The students rushed outside, and Luna, feeling adventurous, decided to follow them into the playground. She watched as the children played on swings and slides, their laughter echoing in the air.

A few brave children began to approach her, offering gentle pats and scratches behind her ears. Luna soaked up the affection, playfully swatting at the swings as they passed by. She felt like a superstar!

As break came to an end, the teacher called everyone back inside. Luna, not wanting the fun to end, jumped up on a nearby windowsill, watching the children with a happy heart. She felt a sense of belonging in this lively place.

When it was time to leave for home, the teacher gently picked Luna up and carried her outside. "Thank you for visiting us, Luna! You're always welcome here," she said with a smile. Luna meowed softly in response, grateful for the wonderful day.

As Luna made her way home, she could not help but think of all the fun she had at school.

Maybe she would become a regular visitor, bringing a little magic and joy to the students' lives!

34

On a misty autumn evening, Luna was exploring a nearby forest, her curiosity leading her more deeply into the woods than usual. The air was crisp, and fallen leaves surrounded her. As she wandered along, she stumbled upon a funny little cottage hidden among the trees, smoke curling from its chimney.

Intrigued, Luna approached the door and, without hesitation, pushed it open with her paw. Inside, she found a warm, cozy space filled with bubbling cauldrons and jars of strange ingredients. At the centre of it all was a kind looking lady witch with wild, brown hair and a twinkle in her eye.

"Well, hello there!" the witch exclaimed, noticing Luna. "A brave little explorer, aren't you?"

Luna tilted her head, intrigued but cautious. The witch chuckled, sensing her curiosity. "Do not worry, dear. I will not bite. I could use a friend to help me with my potions."

With a flick of her wrist, the witch conjured a small treat that landed gently in front of Luna.
 Sniffing it cautiously, Luna decided it was safe enough and took a nibble. It was delicious.

As Luna enjoyed her snack, the witch explained her work. "I am brewing potions to help the forest creatures. "Would you like to help me gather some ingredients?"

Excited by the idea of an adventure, Luna nodded and followed the witch outside. Together, they roamed the woods, collecting mushrooms, herbs, and shining crystals. Luna's keen senses helped her find the rarest items, while the witch shared her wisdom about each ingredient.

As the sun began to set, they returned to the cottage. The witch started mixing the potions, and Luna watched in awe as the ingredients transformed with each stir. "Now, for the final touch," the witch said, adding a sprinkle of moonlight gathered in a tiny vial.

"Do you want to help?" she asked, gesturing to a small jar. Luna leaped onto the counter, ready to assist. With a careful paw, she nudged the jar closer, and together they finished the potion.

With a satisfied grin, the witch poured the potion into small bottles, labelling them with care. "Thank you, Luna! You have been a wonderful assistant. Here is a little something for your help."

The witch handed Luna a tiny, shimmering crystal that glowed softly. "This will bring you good luck and protect you on your adventures."

Luna purred with delight, grateful for the unexpected friendship. As she made her way home, the forest felt even more magical, and she could not wait for her next adventure with the witch!

35

One beautiful afternoon, Luna decided it was the perfect day for a picnic. The sun was shining, the birds were singing, and a gentle breeze danced through the trees. Excitedly, she gathered her friends George the mouse, Grace the Easter bunny, James the wise old owl and the two sister cats -April and November.

"Let's meet at the big oak tree by the pond!" Luna suggested, her green eyes sparkling with enthusiasm. Her friends agreed, and each set off to prepare their favourite treats.

Luna packed a basket with her favourite snacks: crunchy fish-shaped treats, creamy yogurt, and a few delicious catnip biscuits. George brought along some tiny cheese cubes, Grace brought fresh carrot sticks, James carried a selection of berries he had foraged from the nearby bushes, and the sisters brought chicken nibbles.

When they all arrived at the oak tree, they spread out their colourful blanket and set up their feast. "Everything looks amazing!" Luna exclaimed, her tail flicking with excitement.

As they sat down to eat, they chatted and laughed, sharing stories about their adventures. George recounted a daring escape from a curious cat, while Grace shared tales of her speedy hops through the garden. James offered wise advice sprinkled with humour, making everyone chuckle, while April and November shared their adventures of travelling on trains and buses.

After they finished their snacks, Luna had an idea. "How about we play some games? We could have a race or maybe a treasure hunt!"

George's eyes lit up. "A treasure hunt sounds fun! Let us hide something and give clues to finding it!"

The friends agreed, and they quickly each hid a shiny button from Luna's basket. They took turns giving each other clues, and the excitement grew as they searched high and low around the oak tree and the pond.

"Warm, warm, warmer!" Grace called out as George searched under a bush, making everyone giggle.

Finally, Luna spotted a button glinting in the sunlight under a pile of leaves. "I found it!" she shouted, proudly holding it up for all to see. Her friends cheered, and they celebrated with a little dance around the tree.

As the afternoon wore on, they lay back on the blanket, gazing at the clouds drifting lazily across the sky. "This has been the best picnic ever," Luna said, her heart full of joy. "I'm so glad we're friends."

"Me too!" the others chorused.

"Let us do this again soon." With laughter and plans for future picnics, they enjoyed the warm sun and the gentle rustle of leaves, cherishing the special bond they shared. It was a perfect day, filled with friendship, fun, and delicious treats under the big oak tree.

36

One rainy afternoon, Luna noticed that her human dad, Pete, was acting a bit strangely. He was curled up on the sofa, looking pale and tired. Concerned, Luna hopped up beside him, gently nudging his hand with her head.

"Hello," she meowed softly. "What's wrong?"

Pete smiled weakly and scratched behind her ears. "I am just not feeling great today, Luna. I think I might be coming down with a cold."

Luna's instincts kicked in. She had heard stories about how cats could help their humans feel better, and she was determined to take care of Pete. "Do not worry! I will be your nurse," she declared, flicking her tail confidently.

First, Luna jumped down to the kitchen, where she knew Pete kept his favourite snacks. She carefully nudged open the cupboard and managed to push out a small bowl of chicken-flavoured treats. With great effort, she carried it back to the sofa and placed it beside Pete. "Look! I brought you a snack," she said, purring proudly.

Pete chuckled, grateful for her thoughtfulness. "Thanks, Luna. You are a good nurse." He nibbled on a treat, and Luna watched- satisfied that she was helping.

Next, Luna remembered that Pete loved his cozy blanket when he was not feeling well. She hopped back down, dragged the blanket from the armchair, and wrestled with it until it was piled up next to him on the sofa. "Here! You need to stay warm," she insisted.

Pete wrapped the blanket around himself and smiled more brightly. "You are right! This feels nice. Thank you!"

Feeling inspired, Luna then thought about the power of comfort. She settled into a snug spot next to Pete, purring softly. The soothing sound filled the room, creating a calming atmosphere. Luna knew that her presence could bring a sense of comfort to him.

As the rain drummed against the window, Luna stayed by Pete's side, occasionally lifting her head to check on him. She watched him close his eyes and take deep breaths, feeling happy that she could help him relax.

After a while, Pete opened his eyes and looked at Luna. "You know, I think having you here is the best medicine of all," he said, reaching down to give her a gentle scratch behind the ears.

Luna purred even louder, feeling proud of her caregiving skills. "Just doing my job!" she meowed, snuggling closer to him.

As the evening wore on, the rain slowed, and Pete began to feel a little better. Luna stayed by his side, ensuring he had everything he needed: snacks, warmth, and companionship. With her heart full of love, Luna knew that together, they could face anything, even a rainy day filled with colds.

37

One cozy evening, Luna was lounging on the windowsill, watching the sun dip below the horizon. The world outside was slowly settling into the calm of twilight. As the first stars began to twinkle, Luna felt a familiar warmth in her heart.

Just then, her human mum, Susie, entered the room, looking a bit weary after a long day. Luna jumped down from her perch and padded over to her, rubbing against Susie's legs, and purring softly.

"Hey, Luna," Susie said, bending down to give her a gentle scratch behind the ears. "I could use some cuddles tonight."

Luna's ears perked up at the idea. She loved snuggling with Susie! With a joyful leap, she followed Susie to the sofa, where Susie settled in with a warm blanket.

As Susie tucked herself under the blanket, Luna jumped up next to her, curling up in a cozy ball. The soft warmth of Susie's body was the perfect contrast to the cool evening air, and Luna purred contentedly.

"You always know how to make things better," Susie said, stroking Luna's soft fur. "You're my little therapist."

Luna blinked slowly, enjoying the affection. She nudged her head against Susie's hand, urging her to keep petting. As they sat together, the gentle rhythm of Susie's hand on her back felt like the sweetest lullaby.

"Do you want to hear a story?" Susie asked, and Luna perked up, her eyes brightening. She loved listening to Susie's stories, especially the ones filled with adventures and whimsical characters.

As Susie began to weave a tale about a brave little knight and a friendly dragon, Luna listened intently, her purring becoming a soft backdrop to Susie's soothing voice. The world outside faded away, and all that mattered was this moment of warmth and connection.

Eventually, Susie's voice grew quieter, and she felt her eyes getting heavier. "You're the best company, Luna," she whispered, smiling down at her furry friend. Luna responded with a gentle nuzzle, and purred "I'm here for you."

As the stars twinkled outside and the room grew dim, Susie drifted off to sleep, the warmth of Luna by her side bringing her comfort. Luna curled up closer, feeling a sense of peace wash over her. Together, they embraced the quiet magic of the evening- two friends snuggled up against the world, ready to dream of new adventures.

38

One sunny afternoon, Luna was enjoying a peaceful nap when suddenly, she heard a strange sound coming from the bathroom. It was splashing and bubbling, and her curiosity was instantly piqued.

With a flick of her tail, Luna padded toward the bathroom, her ears perked up. As she peeked inside, she saw her Susie, filling the bathtub with water. Bubbles floated on the surface, and the whole scene looked quite inviting except for one little detail: Luna had never liked water.

"Uh-oh," Luna thought, stepping cautiously into the bathroom. "What's going on in here?"

Susie noticed her and smiled. "Hey, Luna! I am just getting ready for a bath. Want to come, and see?"

Luna hesitated. The thought of water made her a little scared. "I think I'll just watch from a safe distance," she meowed, sitting at the doorway, her tail twitching.

As Susie added some lavender-scented bubbles to the bath, the room filled with a lovely fragrance.

Luna's curiosity began to outweigh her caution. She stepped closer, drawn in by the sweet scent and the way the bubbles danced in the light.

"See? It is nice!" Susie said, reaching down to give Luna a gentle scratch behind the ears. "You could even join me if you wanted to."

Luna flicked her ears back at the idea. "Join you in the water? Not a chance!" she meowed, wrinkling her nose playfully. But the allure of the bubbles was hard to resist. Maybe just a little closer would not hurt.

As Susie settled into the bath, Luna could not help but hop up onto the edge of the tub, her paws just inches from the water. She leaned in to sniff the bubbles, and to her surprise, they smelled delightful.

Suddenly, one of the bubbles popped, and Luna jumped back with a startled meow! Susie laughed, splashing a little water toward her. "It's just a bubble, silly!"

With a mix of curiosity and caution, Luna decided to stay close. She watched as Susie played with the bubbles, creating tiny floating orbs that danced across the surface. The sound of water splashing was relaxing, and Luna found herself feeling a little braver.

After a while, Susie invited her again. "Come on, Luna! Just dip your paw in. It is not so bad!"

With a deep breath, Luna inched forward and gently dipped one paw into the warm water. To her surprise, it felt nice! She pulled her paw back and gave it a shake, then took a moment to think.

"Okay, maybe this isn't the worst thing ever," she admitted, slowly inching closer again. With newfound courage, she decided to join Susie by jumping up to the edge of the tub, her paws just brushing the surface.

"You're doing great!" Susie cheered. Luna purred, feeling proud of her little adventure. The bubbles continued to pop and dance, and for the first time, Luna found herself enjoying the experience.

As bathtime continued, Susie pushed the bubbles gentle towards Luna. The playful kitty could not resist the temptation; she swatted at the bubbles, watching them burst with delight.

By the end of the bath, Luna was no longer just an observer. She had discovered that maybe, just maybe, water was not so scary after all. And as Susie dried off, Luna realized that she had faced her fears and had a little fun in the process.

From that day on, the bathroom was not just a place of splashes, it was a space of playful memories, and Luna found herself looking forward to the next bath- bubbles, and all!

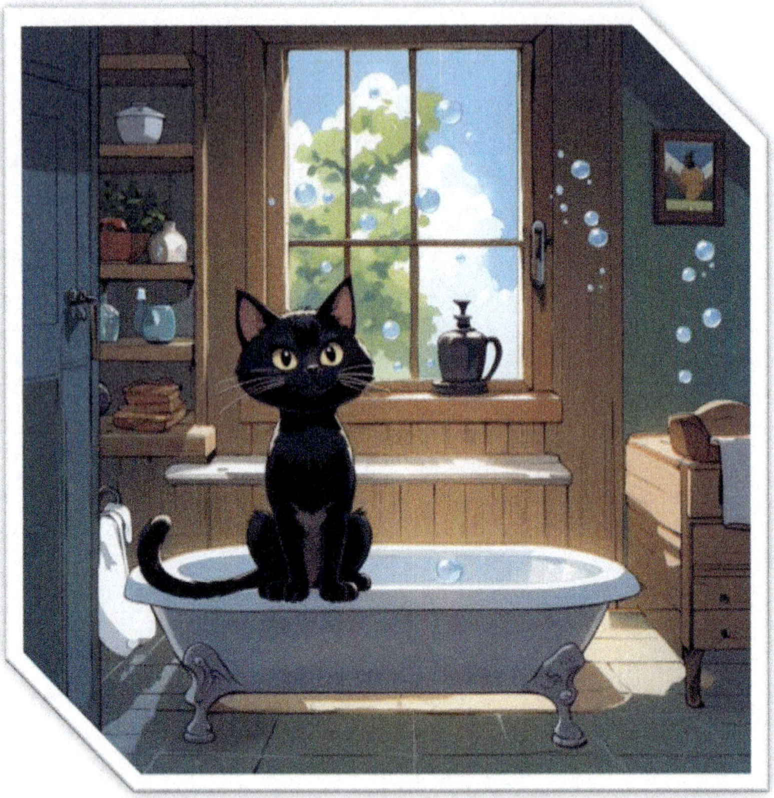

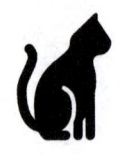

39

One cold afternoon, Luna decided to visit Mandy who lived just a few houses down. Mandy always had exciting stories to share, and Luna was eager to visit her.

With a flick of her tail, Luna set off on her journey, padding down the path and through the garden gates until she reached Mandy's front door. Luna gently tapped her paw on the door, and to her delight, it swung open.

"Mandy!" Luna meowed; her eyes bright with excitement. "It's me!"

Mandy's face lit up with a big smile. "Luna! I am so glad you came to visit!" She bent down to give Luna a gentle scratch behind her ears. "Come in! I have something special to show you."

Luna trotted inside, her whiskers twitching with curiosity. The room was filled with colourful toys, art supplies, and books stacked high on every surface. But what caught Luna's attention was a big cardboard box in the corner.

"What's in there?" Luna asked, tilting her head.

Mandy giggled. "It is a surprise! I was going to make a fort for Daisy, Trigg, and Misty. Want to help me?"

Luna's eyes sparkled with delight. "Of course! Let us build a fantastic fort!" Together, they set to work, stacking pillows and blankets, and draping them over the box to create a cozy hideout.

Once their fort was finished, Mandy crawled inside with the four cats, surrounded by soft, colourful fabric. Mandy pulled out a book and began to read them a story about brave adventurers exploring magical lands. Luna curled up beside her, purring softly, completely engrossed in the tale.

When the story ended, Mandy declared: "Time for a snack!"

"Oh, perfect! we love snacks!" Luna, Daisy, Trigg, and Misty exclaimed, following Mandy into the kitchen. There, Mandy ate a plate of crunchy apple slices and peanut butter, while Luna, Daisy, Trigg and Misty enjoyed a few cats' treats. As they ate, they shared stories and laughter, enjoying the delicious food together.

As the afternoon began to fade into evening, Luna knew it was time to head home. "Thank you for such a wonderful day, Mandy!" she purred, her heart full of joy.

Mandy beamed. "Let us do it again soon! "

With a final nuzzle and a happy meow, Luna set off back home, already dreaming of their next playdate. She had found a true friend in Mandy, and together, they had created magical memories that would last a lifetime.

40

One quiet evening, Luna was lounging on the windowsill, basking in the warm glow of the setting sun. Her peaceful evening was interrupted by a strange figure sneaking around the garden next door. Intrigued, Luna perked up, her green eyes narrowing as she watched a shadowy silhouette dart from bush to bush.

The figure was a jewel thief, known for their quick movements and clever tricks. He was looking for a way to break into the house rumoured to hold a valuable collection of jewels. Unbeknownst to him, Luna was not just any ordinary cat; she was a watchful guardian of the homes in her neighbourhood.

As the thief crept closer, Luna decided to investigate. She leaped down from the windowsill and padded silently across the yard. With a flick of her tail, she darted behind a flowerpot, her instincts on high alert.

Suddenly, the thief heard a rustle. "What was that?" he whispered, glancing around nervously. Luna, her heart racing, remained still, blending into the shadows. The thief shrugged it off and continued his approach.

Just as he was about to reach the side door, Luna decided to make her presence known. With a loud meow, she jumped into the thief's path. Startled, the thief stumbled back, nearly dropping his bag of tools. "What the?" he exclaimed.

Luna took this opportunity to hiss playfully- her fur bristling as she approached with a mix of curiosity and defiance. The thief, now more focused on the unexpected feline than his mission, hesitated, unsure of what to do next.

Just then, June stepped out onto the porch with Archie at her side, drawn by the commotion. "Luna? What is going on?" she called out, her voice cutting through the night air. The thief's eyes widened, realizing he had been caught. With a quick glance at Luna, he turned and sprinted away, vanishing into the darkness.

Her neighbour June rushed over to Luna, who was proudly standing her ground. "You scared them off!" she said, kneeling to give her a gentle scratch behind the ears. Luna purred loudly, loving the attention and the thrill of the moment.

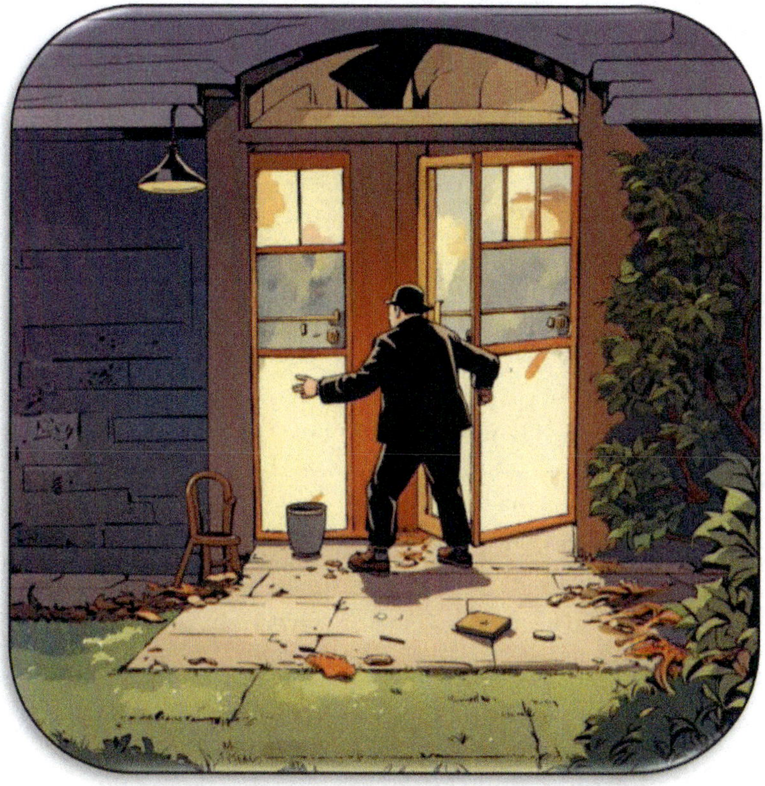

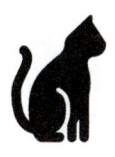

41

One sunny morning, Luna was exploring her garden-

enjoying the scent of blooming flowers and the warmth of the sun on her fur. As she wandered around, she suddenly heard a frantic chirping coming from a nearby bush. Curiosity piqued; she padded over to investigate.

There, among the leaves, she found a little bird flapping its wings in distress. "Oh no, what's wrong?" Luna meowed; her green eyes wide with concern.

The little bird looked up at her with teary eyes. "I fell out of my nest, and I cannot find my way back! My mum is going to be so worried!" it chirped.

Luna's heart went out to the little bird. "Do not worry! I will help you find your nest," she declared confidently. "Can you remember where it was?"

The little bird thought hard. "It was in a tree near the big garden with the flowers and lots of trees, but I don't remember which one!"

"Let's start there!" Luna said, her determination shining through. Together, they set off toward the big garden. As they walked, Luna reassured the little bird, "We will find it! Just stick with me."

When they reached the garden, Luna scanned the trees with her sharp eyes. "There are so many! Can you remember what your nest looked like?"

The little bird chirped again. "It was cozy and made of twigs, and it had soft feathers inside!"

Luna led the way, checking each tree carefully. She approached the first one, peering into the branches. "Is this it?" she asked, but the nest was empty.

"No, that's not it," the little bird replied, looking worried. "What if I can't find my mum again?"

"Don't worry," Luna said gently. "We will keep looking! Let us try the next tree."

They moved from tree to tree, and after a few tries, they came to a tall oak tree. As Luna looked up, her heart skipped a beat. There, nestled in the branches, was a small nest that looked just like the one the little bird had described.

"Is that it?" Luna asked, her voice full of excitement.

"Yes! That is, it!" the little bird chirped, flapping its wings in joy. "That's my home!"

With a determined leap, Luna climbed onto the lowest branch of the tree. "Okay, I can't reach it, but I can help you up!"

The little bird fluttered up, gaining confidence. It hopped from branch to branch, and with a final flap, it landed safely in the nest. It looked around, chirping happily. "I am home! Thank you, Luna!"

Luna purred with joy, watching the little bird settle in. Just then, a larger bird appeared, flying in with a worm in its beak. The little bird chirped excitedly, and the larger bird cooed softly, clearly relieved to see its little one safe.

"I couldn't have done it without you!" the little bird chirped, looking down at Luna with gratitude. "You're my hero!"

Luna felt a warm glow in her heart. "I am just glad I could help. Remember, you can always count on friends!"

As she watched the bird family reunited, Luna felt happy knowing she had made a difference. With a gentle flick of her tail, she turned to head back home, her heart full of warmth and the joy of helping a friend in need.

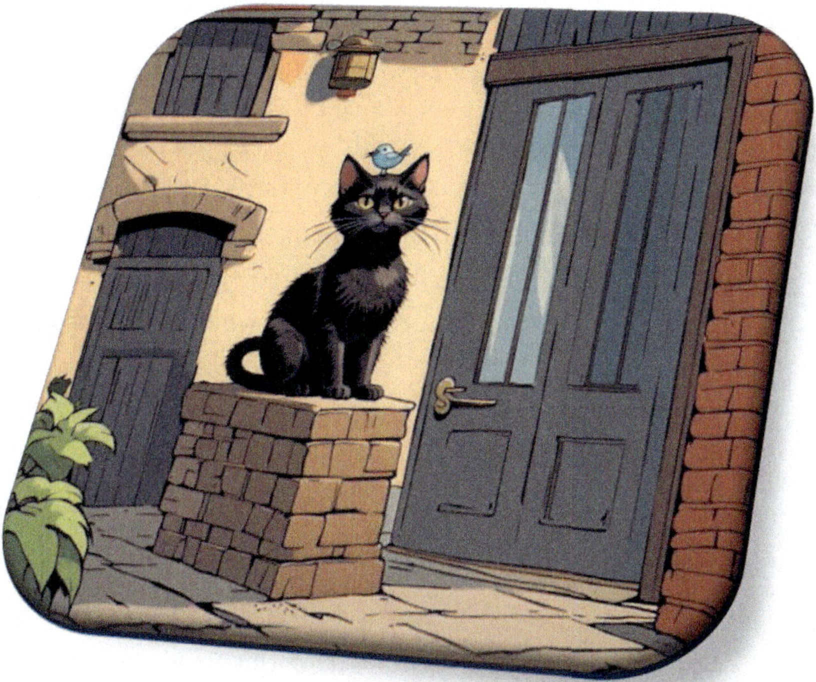

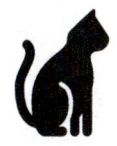

42

Luna was curled up on her cozy spot on the sofa enjoying the sound of raindrops tapping against the window, while her human dad, Pete, was preparing for a movie night.

"Tonight's feature is a classic scary film!" Pete announced, settling in with popcorn and a blanket. Luna's ears perked up at the word "scary." While she had never seen a scary movie before, she was curious about what all the fuss was about.

As the movie started, the room was filled with eerie music and dim lighting. Luna perched herself on the armrest, her eyes wide as she watched the screen. She found herself inching closer to Pete, who happily munched on popcorn.

Suddenly, a loud crash echoed from the screen, and a figure jumped out of the darkness. Luna leaped backwards with a startled yowl, her fur bristling. "What was that?!" she meowed, her heart racing.

Pete chuckled, reaching over to give her a reassuring scratch behind the ears. "It is just a movie, Luna. Nothing to fear!"

Luna took a deep breath, trying to calm her racing heart. "Right... just a movie," she meowed, though she remained on high alert, her eyes darting back to the screen. The suspense continued to build, and Luna found herself both intrigued and terrified.

As the story unfolded, she watched as the characters faced all sorts of spooky situations. Every creak and whisper made her jump, but there was something thrilling about it too. Luna could not help but feel a rush of excitement mixed with her fear.

At one particularly tense moment, a ghostly figure appeared out of nowhere. Luna let out a surprised squeak, leaping off the armrest and landing on Pete's lap, her little heart pounding, her wide eyes locked on the screen.

Pete laughed softly, stroking her fur. "You can hide if you want, Luna. It is just pretend."

Luna thought for a moment but then realized that being scared was part of the fun. She took a deep breath and climbed back onto the armrest, determined to face the scary movie head-on. "Okay, I can do this!" she declared, puffing out her chest.

As the movie reached its climax, Luna found herself so engaged that she forgot to be scared. She was entranced by the plot twists and clever surprises. Each of her jumps became mixed with feelings of thrills and excitement. By the time the credits rolled, Luna was ready to pounce off the couch in excitement rather than fright.

"That was… intense!" she meowed, her heart still racing, "Can we watch another one?"

Pete grinned, surprised by her newfound bravery. "Sure! How about a spooky comedy instead?"

Luna's eyes lit up. "Yes, please! Let us keep the fun going!"

And so, as the rain continued to fall outside, Luna settled back in, ready for laughter and thrills, feeling proud of herself for facing her fears. She discovered that sometimes, the scariest things could lead to the most entertaining adventures, especially when shared with a friend.

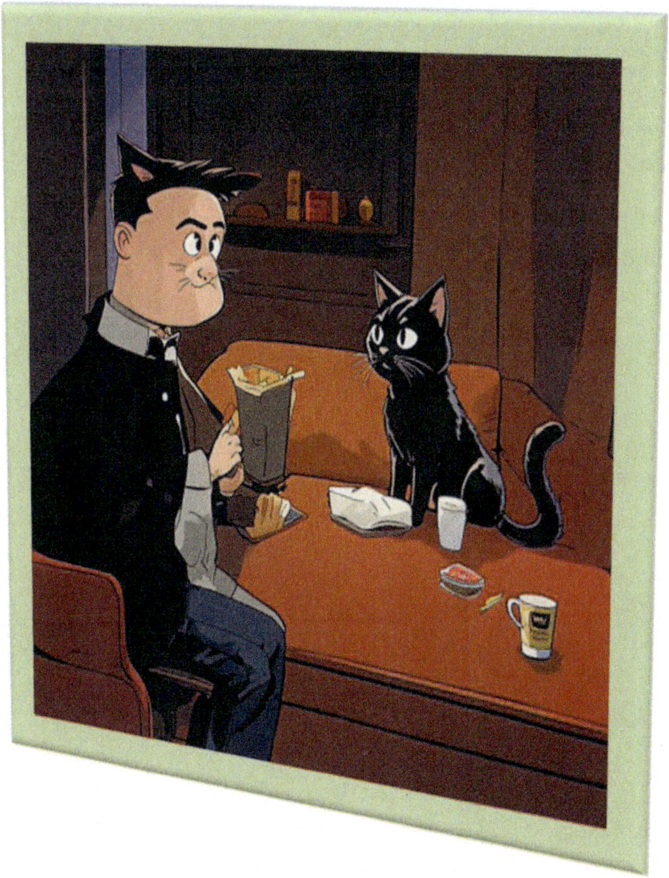

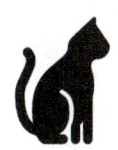

43

Luna found herself feeling adventurous. As she roamed around the garden, she spotted an enticing bird perched on a high branch of a nearby tree. With her natural feline curiosity, she could not resist the urge to climb up for a closer look.

She scampered up the trunk, her claws digging into the bark. But once she reached the branch where the bird had been, she realized it had flown away! Suddenly aware of how high she had climbed, Luna's confidence wavered. Looking down, she felt a flutter of panic she was much higher than she had intended.

Just then, June, who had been tending to her garden nearby, noticed Luna's predicament. "Luna! What are you doing up there?" she called out, concern creeping into her voice.

Luna meowed softly, her big green eyes wide as she took in the distance from the ground. June approached the tree, her heart racing a little. "Hang tight, I'll help you!"

With calm determination, June grabbed a sturdy ladder from the shed and propped it against the tree. She climbed up carefully, calling to Luna in a soothing tone. "You are okay girl! Just a little further!"

Luna watched, her anxiety slowly fading as she recognized June's familiar voice. When June reached her, she extended a hand gently. "Come on, Luna. You can do it!"

With a tentative leap, Luna hopped into June's arms, purring with relief. June chuckled, hugging her tightly. "See? That was not so bad, was it?"

As they descended the ladder together, Luna felt grateful for her friend's help, realizing that sometimes, adventures could lead to unexpected challenges. Once safely on the ground, Luna nuzzled against June's leg, grateful to be back on solid ground and ready for a new kind of adventure- one that did not involve climbing trees!

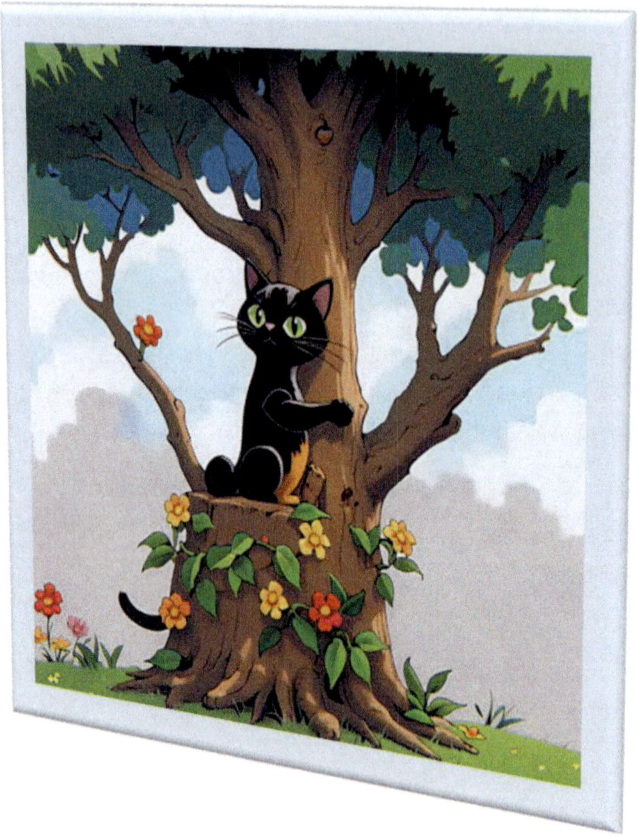

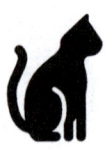

44

Holly was feeling sad as she walked through the quaint streets of her neighbourhood, her mind wandering with thoughts of finding a job. She loved baking, but getting a job was proving impossible. Just then, she spotted her friend Luna- the playful black cat who belonged to her neighbours Susie and Pete. Luna was lounging in a sunbeam, her glossy coat shimmering in the light.

"Hey there, Luna," Holly said, as she knelt down to scratch behind the cat's ears. "I could really use your help. I need a job, and I just do not know where to start."

Luna purred and with a mischievous glint in her eyes, she darted down the street, pausing to glance back at Holly and meowed: "Follow me!"

Curious and amused, Holly followed Luna as she led her to "Sweet Delights," the charming local cake shop with the sweetest aroma wafting from its doors. Holly had always dreamed of working there, but had not gathered the courage to apply.

With a gentle nudge, Luna guided Holly toward the entrance. "Alright girl, time to seize the day!" Holly said to herself, taking a deep breath. Just as she approached the door, Mrs. Eastwood, the shop owner, stepped outside.

"Hello there!" Mrs. Eastwood said, smiling warmly. "Are you looking for something?"

Holly blurted out, "I would love to apply for a job here! I am passionate about baking and would be thrilled and honoured to work with you."

Luna sat proudly at Holly's feet, as if she were Holly's secret weapon. Mrs. Eastwood chuckled at the sight of the confident cat. "Well, it seems you have a furry friend backing you up! We could always use some extra help in the kitchen. Would you like to come in for a chat?"

Holly's heart soared. After a delightful conversation about cakes, recipes, and the joy of baking, Mrs. Eastwood offered her a part-time position. Holly could hardly believe it.

"Thank you so much!" Holly exclaimed, glancing down at Luna, who purred in approval.

As they walked home together, Holly felt a rush of excitement. "We did it, Luna! You really helped me!"

From that day on, Luna was Holly's lucky charm- always nearby while she baked, and brought smiles to everyone at Sweet Delights. Their friendship deepened, and Holly knew she could always count on her clever feline friend to guide her through life's challenges.

45

Luna was filled with excitement as she prepared for her trip to Braunton, Devon, to visit Aunty Anne and Uncle Mike. The journey was a new experience for her, but she loved adventures, especially when it meant meeting family.

As they arrived, Luna peeked out of her carrier, her big green eyes wide with curiosity. Aunty Anne greeted them with open arms and a warm smile, while Uncle Mike chuckled, saying, "Let's see what our little guest thinks of her new surroundings!"

Once inside their cozy home, Luna immediately began to explore. The living room was filled with delightful smells, and a sunbeam streaming through the window caught her attention. She made a beeline for it, stretching out to soak in the warmth.

Aunty Anne had prepared a special spot for Luna, complete with a soft blanket and some fishy treats. As Luna settled in, Uncle Mike brought out a few toys, and soon they were playing together. Luna chased after a feather toy, darting around the room, and bringing laughter to everyone.

The days in Braunton were filled with strolls along the village streets, where Luna enjoyed watching the world go by from her little backpack carrier. Aunty Anne and Uncle Mike introduced her to their lovely garden, where Luna chased butterflies and lounged in the grass.

One evening, as they gathered around the fireplace, Aunty Anne shared stories from her own childhood, while Uncle Mike made sure Luna had plenty of treats. Luna curled up in Aunty Anne's lap, purring contentedly, feeling like a cherished part of the family.

As the visit came to an end, Luna realized she had made wonderful memories in Braunton, filled with love and laughter. She would always look forward to her next adventure with Aunty Anne and Uncle Mike, knowing they would welcome her with open arms.

46

Lounging in her favourite spot by the window, Luna heard a commotion outside. Curious, she hopped down and padded to the door, where she spotted her human mum and dad in the garden.

"Hey, Luna!" Pete called, waving at her. "Come join us!"

But Luna hesitated, her mind racing. She remembered the strange smell she had detected in the house- something smoky and unsettling. "Pete! Susie!" Luna meowed urgently, rushing outside. "Come quickly!"

Susie crouched down; her eyes wide. "What is it, Luna?"

"Theres a fire in your room, Susie! I smelled smoke!" Luna meowed, her fur bristling with concern.

Susie's face paled. "A fire? Are you sure?" Luna nodded. "Yes! It was coming from the corner of your room. You need to check!"

Without a moment to lose, Pete and Susie dashed toward the house, with Luna leading the way. They hurried into Susie's room, and Susie gasped as she saw wisps of smoke rising from her bedside lamp, which had overheated.

"Oh no!" Susie cried. "We have to turn it off!"

"Quickly!" Luna urged, her heart racing. Susie flicked the switch off, and the smoke began to disappear. Pete opened the window to let some fresh air in, while Luna stood watch, her eyes alert for any sign of danger.

"Luna, thank you for telling us!" Pete said, his voice filled with relief. "If you hadn't, who knows what could have happened?"

Susie knelt to give Luna a gentle scratch behind the ears. "Thank you so much, Luna! You saved the day!"

Feeling a warm glow of pride, Luna purred softly. "I just wanted to keep you safe. I did not like the smell, and I knew something was wrong."

After checking the room thoroughly to make sure everything was safe, they all took a deep breath, relieved that the situation had not turned worse. Susie turned to her and Pete and said "We need to be more careful. I will get a new lamp that has an automatic shut-off feature!"

"Great idea!" Pete agreed. "And we should make sure to check all the electrical sockets and cords regularly."

With the crisis averted, Luna meowed "Let's celebrate by having some treats!" she suggested, her spirits lifting.

They all headed to the kitchen, where Susie set out some snacks. As they enjoyed their goodies, Luna shared stories about other adventures she had experienced.

The memory of the scare from earlier faded, replaced by laughter.

That day, Luna learned the importance of being vigilant and the power of teamwork.

47

Susie was having a busy afternoon, balancing her writing while eating a snack, when she accidentally knocked over a glass of water. It spilled right onto the electrical sockets by her desk, sending a jolt of panic through her. "Oh no!" she exclaimed, quickly grabbing a towel to wipe up the mess.

Meanwhile, Luna, perched on her favourite windowsill, watched the commotion unfold. With a graceful leap, Luna hopped down and padded over to Susie, her keen eyes taking in the scene.

As Susie frantically tried to clean up, Luna nudged a dry towel towards her with her paw, guiding it towards the wet area. "Thank you, Luna!" Susie said, chuckling at her furry companion's helpfulness. With the second towel in place, Susie managed to soak up the excess water.

Then, Luna noticed the electrical sockets still glistening with moisture. She darted over to a nearby drawer and pawed at it until Susie opened it, revealing some old rags. Susie smiled, realizing what Luna was suggesting. "You are right! I need to be more careful!"

Together, they worked quickly. Susie wiped the sockets dry while Luna kept a watchful eye, making sure everything was safe. Once the area was dry, Susie let out a sigh of relief and gave Luna a gentle scratch behind her ears. "Thanks for the help, Luna. You really are my little hero!"

Feeling proud of her teamwork, Luna settled back down in her sunny spot, content that she had played a part in keeping Susie safe.

48

In loving memory of Loki April 2016 - November 2023

Luna had been dreaming of a picnic under the ancient oak tree at the edge of the park. The tree stood like a sentinel over the rolling hills, its gnarled branches providing a perfect canopy for shade. She scampered around the house, her slender tail flicking with excitement as Susie packed a wicker basket with all their favourites: freshly baked scones, strawberries, and a thermos of tea.

As they made their way to the oak tree, Luna suddenly felt a tingle in the air. A chill swept through her fur, and she looked up to see a faint, shimmering figure floating among the branches- it was Loki, the resident ghost cat, known for his mischievous spirit and enchanting tales of the supernatural.

Loki had long been a friend to Luna, and he loved to play pranks on unsuspecting wanderers of the woods. His shimmering coat was more transparent than tangible, shifting between shades of blue and silver as sunlight filtered through the leaves. Luna meowed excitedly, and Loki glided down gracefully, his ghostly tail trailing behind him like a wisp of smoke.

"What brings you to my domain, Luna?" he purred, a twinkle in his ghostly eyes. "Are you planning some mortal celebration without me?"

"Of course not!" Luna replied, her voice bubbling with joy. "We are having a picnic, and you are invited! Join us!"

With that, the trio settled beneath the sprawling branches of the oak. Susie, blissfully unaware of Loki's ghostly nature, spread a colourful checkered blanket and began to lay out their delightful spread. Luna, delighted to have both her dear friend and the spirited Loki alongside her, felt a sense of happiness swell in her chest.

As they feasted, Loki entertained them with stories of the past of ancient cat legends, lost treasures, and the laughter of the wind on moonlit nights. Luna listened intently, dreaming of one day going on a grand adventure herself. Eventually, as laughter and chatter filled the air, Loki suddenly swished his transparent paw and conjured a burst of shimmering light, creating playful illusions of butterflies dancing around them.

Susie giggled, trying to catch the ethereal creatures with her hands, blissfully unaware that the real magic was sitting right beside her, his spirit swirling with laughter. Suddenly, Loki had an idea. "Why don't we make this picnic even more adventurous? Let us explore the Enchanted Glade."

"What's the Enchanted Glade?" Luna asked, her eyes wide with curiosity.

"It's a hidden place just beyond the oak tree, filled with wonders and whispers of the forest's oldest secrets!" Loki explained, hopping excitedly. "Only those with true hearts can find it."

With hearts brimming with excitement, Luna and Susie followed Loki, who twinkled as he led the way, floating above the ground. They meandered through twists and turns until they arrived at the entrance of a mystical glade, filled with beautiful flowers that sparkled in a spectrum of colours, and ancient trees that illuminated the twilight with their soft glow.

As they entered, Luna felt a surge of energy. The flowers swayed to a melody only the wind could hear, and fireflies danced around them, painting a tableau of light. With Loki's guidance, they discovered hidden treasures: a tiny pond that reflected their laughter, a grove where wisps of fog seemed to play, and a patch of grass that tickled their feet as they ran.

As the sun began to set, painting the sky in hues of pink and gold, they returned to their picnic spot, their hearts filled to the brim with memories of their adventure. Susie smiled at Luna, and though she never quite understood how their day had been so magical, she felt grateful for every moment.

Luna, with her heart full of joy and new tales of wonder, curled up beside Susie, looking up to the shimmering sky. Loki floated above them, his spirit ever watchful, knowing that the bond of friendship was the greatest adventure of all.

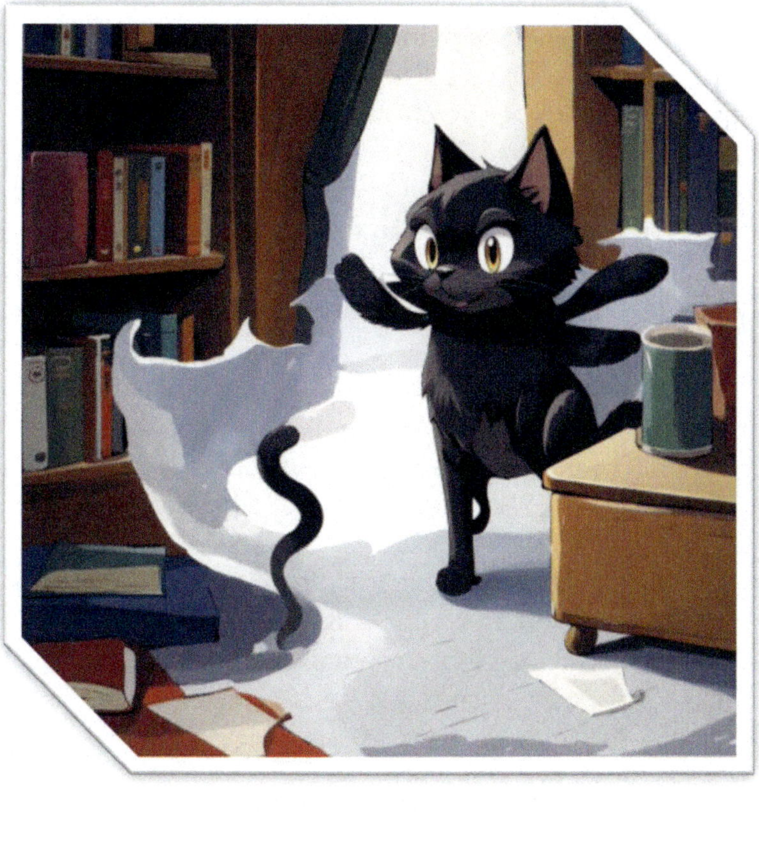

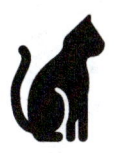

49

Luna, stretched lazily in the sunbeam streaming through the window before deciding it was time to visit her friend Di in Bourton-on-the-Water. With a flick of her tail, she hopped off her perch and trotted to the door.

Upon arriving at Di's cozy cottage, Luna padded up to the door and gave a gentle meow. Di opened the door, her face lighting up at the sight of Luna. "There you are, my lovely!" she exclaimed, scooping Luna up for a warm hug.

Inside, the two settled into the living room, where Di had set out a comfy blanket just for Luna. After a quick snack of treats, Luna explored the nooks and crannies of Di's home, her curious nose twitching at all the new scents.

Once Luna had satisfied her curiosity, Di suggested a stroll along the riverbank. Luna followed Di outside, her little paws padding softly on the cobblestone paths. The quaint charm of Bourton-on-the-Water surrounded them as they wandered, with Luna occasionally pausing to watch the ducks or bat at the fluttering leaves.

As the sun began to dip, casting a golden glow over the village, Di and Luna found a quiet spot to sit by the water. Luna curled up in Di's lap, purring contentedly as they enjoyed the peaceful evening together. It was the perfect day filled with friendship, exploration, and warmth.

50

Luna, was lounging in her favourite spot in the garden when Josie rushed by, her eyes wide with worry. "Luna, I can't find Slippy!" she exclaimed, referring to her beloved pet snake. Luna perked up, hearing the sadness in Josie's voice.

With a flick of her tail, Luna jumped down and followed Josie. The sun was shining, but Josie's worried expression cast a shadow over the beautiful day. "He was just here in the garden, and now he's gone!" she said, scanning the area.

Luna, always curious, started her search by sniffing around the flower beds. She prowled through the tall grass, her keen senses on alert. After a few moments of investigating, she noticed a trail in the soil leading towards the garden shed.

Josie followed closely behind as Luna led the way. When they reached the shed, Luna paused, her ears perked up. She peered inside, her green eyes reflecting the dim light. "Slippy? Are you in there?" Josie called softly.

With a gentle nudge from Luna, Josie opened the shed door wider, and there, curled up in a cozy corner, was Slippy, basking in the warmth of the sun streaming through a crack. "There you are!" Josie exclaimed, relief washing over her as she scooped up her snake.

Luna meowed proudly, having played her part in the rescue. Josie scratched her behind the ears, grinning. "Thanks, Luna! You are the best detective!" Luna purred in response, happy to have helped her friend and reuniting her with Slippy. The three of them spent the rest of the afternoon playing and enjoying the sunshine, a perfect end to their little adventure.

51

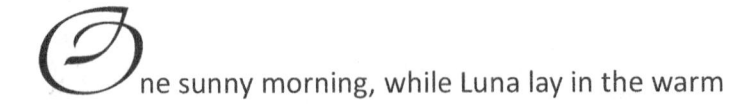

One sunny morning, while Luna lay in the warm morning sun, Susie and Pete walked into the room holding her carrier. "Luna, we need to go to the vet today," they said gently.

Luna's ears perked up. "The vet? Why?" she meowed, her green eyes wide with curiosity and a touch of worry. "You need to get your vaccination," Susie explained, kneeling to scratch Luna behind her ears. "It's important for your health, but I know it can be a little scary."

Luna was not sure how she felt about that. She had heard stories from her friends about the vet- a place that smelled funny and had strange machines and noises. "What if I don't want to go?" she meowed softly.

Pete smiled reassuringly. "We be right there with you. And remember, the vet is only looking out for you. It will be over before you know it."

With a little huff, Luna reluctantly hopped down from the windowsill.

She knew they were right; it was important to stay healthy. So, with a flick of her tail, she followed them to the door.

Once they arrived at the veterinary clinic, Luna felt her heart race. The waiting room was filled with the sounds of barking dogs and the occasional meow from other cats. "See? It is not so bad," Susie said, giving her a reassuring pat.

They took a seat, and Luna watched as other pets came and went. A friendly dog wagged his tail and came over to say hello. "Don't worry, it'll be quick!" he barked cheerfully.

Just then, the receptionist called, "Luna?"

Susie and Pete stood up, holding Luna close. "That's us!" Susie said, and they followed the vet into the examination room.

Inside, the vet, a kind woman with a gentle smile, greeted them. "Hello, Luna! I hear you are here for your vaccination. You are going to do great!"

Luna was not so sure, but she liked the vet's calm voice. Pete sat down on a chair, holding Luna close, and the vet began to examine her gently. "You're a very healthy girl!" she said, checking Luna's ears and feeling her fur. Luna relaxed a little, feeling her human's reassuring presence.

"Now, we just have to give you a quick injection, and then you can have a treat!" the vet said, preparing the needle. Luna's heart raced again, but she took a deep breath, focusing on Susie's soothing words: "Just a little pinch, and then it'll be all over," she said, stroking Luna's back. "You're so brave!"

And just like that, it was done. Luna barely felt the needle, and before she knew it, the vet was giving her a little treat. "See? You did it!" the vet cheered, and Luna felt a surge of pride.

Once they were done, Luna hopped down, feeling relieved and accomplished. "You were amazing!" the vet said, giving her a loving scratch. "We are so proud of you."

As they headed home, Luna could not help but feel a sense of triumph. The vet visit had turned out to be much better than she had anticipated. She snuggled up to Susie on the sofa, her heart full of happiness. "I did it!" Luna purred contentedly. "And I even got a treat!"

Susie and Pete laughed, wrapping their arms around Luna. "Yes, you did! And now you are all set for a healthy future. We knew you could do it."

With that, Luna settled in for a cozy nap, dreaming of her next adventure knowing she was brave and strong, and that the vet was just part of keeping her healthy and happy.

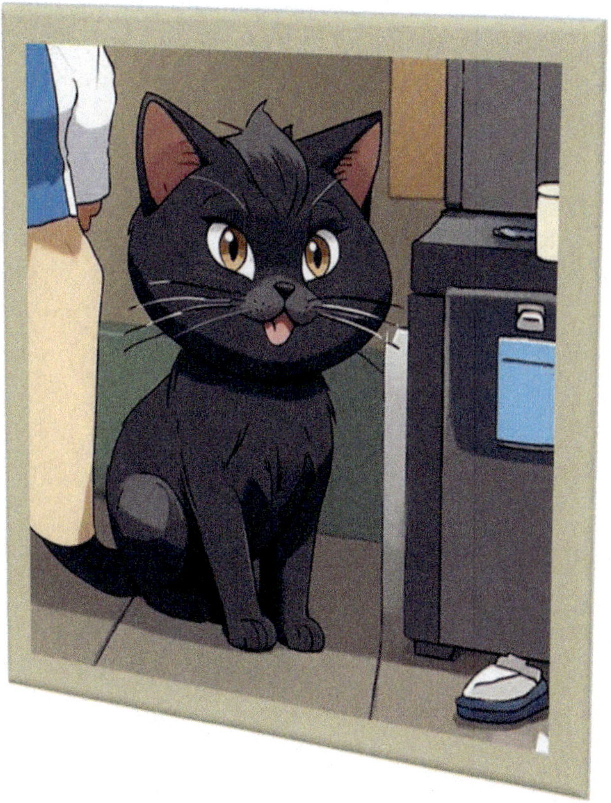

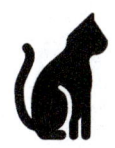

52

Luna had her sights set on the Christmas tree the moment it was decorated. The twinkling lights and shiny ornaments were a playground just waiting to be explored. She would crouch down, tail flicking, ready to pounce on the dangling ornaments.

One evening, as the family gathered around, Luna could not resist any longer. She made her leap, sending a cascade of ornaments clattering to the floor. The room erupted in laughter, and Luna, undeterred, sat proudly among the chaos, "What? I was just helping with the festivities!" she meowed

From that day on, the tree became her favourite spot.

Luna brought a special kind of magic to the holiday season, turning every moment into a delightful adventure.

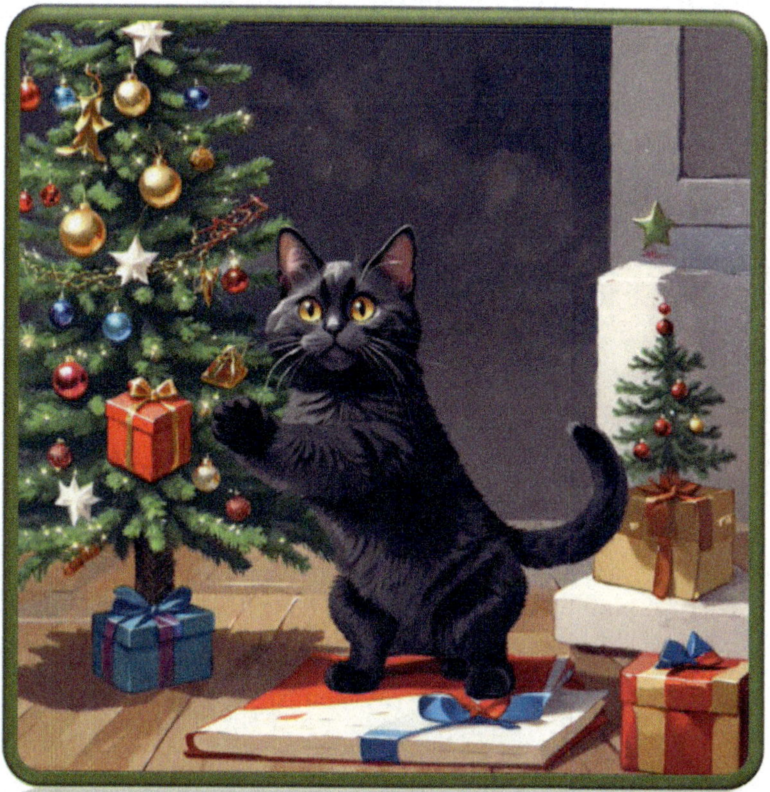

53

On the night of Christmas Eve, as the snow blanketed the ground, Luna sat by the window, watching the world outside. She had heard stories of Father Christmas, and her curiosity was piqued. Would he really come to visit?

As the clock struck midnight, Luna's ears perked up at the sound of soft footsteps on the roof. Suddenly, the chimney shook, and there he appeared- a jolly figure, his red suit bright against the darkness. Father Christmas had arrived!

Luna, intrigued and a little cautious, padded softly towards him. Father Christmas knelt, his eyes twinkling behind his spectacles. "Well, what do we have here?" he said with a chuckle, holding out a festive catnip toy.

With a playful swat, Luna grabbed the toy and rolled onto her back. Father Christmas laughed, clearly charmed by the spirited cat. "Looks like you've been a good little girl this year," he said, glancing at the pile of gifts he had brought.

After sharing a few moments of playful interaction, Father Christmas filled Luna's stocking with treats and toys, whispering, "For the one who brings joy to everyone." With a wink and a hearty laugh, he bid Luna farewell and made his way back up the chimney.

As the first light of dawn broke, Luna awoke to find her new toys and treats, her heart full of the magic of the night. She knew that this Christmas would be one to remember, thanks to her unexpected meeting with Father Christmas.

54

On Christmas morning, Luna woke up to the smell of pine needles and warmth filling the house.

As the family gathered around, Luna watched eagerly as they began to unwrap gifts. The excitement in the room was noticeable, and her curiosity peaked when she spotted a brightly wrapped box labelled just for her. With a little nudge, she pushed her way to the front, her tail flicking with joy.

Once the box was opened, out tumbled an array of delightful toys- feather wands, crinkly balls, and even a little plush mouse that squeaked! Luna's eyes widened with joy as she batted at the toys, sending the plush mouse skittering across the floor. She leapt after it, her playful spirit shining through.

But that was not all. Beneath the tree was a festive stocking filled with treats. As the family watched, Luna dived into it, her little paws rummaging through the goodies. There were catnip toys, crunchy treats, and even a special tuna snack that she could not resist.

With each new toy and treat, Luna's excitement grew, turning the living room into a playground. She dashed around, her new feather wand trailing behind her, and then settled down with her favourite toy, purring contentedly.

The laughter and joy of the day wrapped around her like a warm blanket. Luna knew that this Christmas was special not just for the toys and treats, but for the love that filled the room, making her feel like the happiest cat in the world.

55

After a day filled with excitement and adventures, Luna returned home- her paws a little weary but her heart full of joy. She had explored the park, made new friends, and even helped a lost bird find its way back to its nest. As she padded through the door, she let out a contented sigh, grateful for the day's experiences.

The sun was beginning to set, casting a warm golden glow across the living room. Luna stretched her legs and yawned widely, her little pink tongue flicking out. She knew just the perfect spot for a long, cozy nap.

Luna trotted over to her favourite blanket, on the sofa. It was soft and smelled faintly of sunshine. With a happy purr, she circled a few times, then settled down into the fluffy fabric, tucking her paws beneath her.

As she closed her eyes, her mind drifted back to the day's adventures. She remembered the sound of laughter, the rustle of leaves, and the feeling of the warm sun on her fur. A smile crept across her face as she thought about her new friends and the fun they had shared.

Soon, the rhythmic sound of her purring filled the room, blending with the gentle rustle of leaves outside. The world outside faded away as Luna slipped into a deep sleep, dreaming of chasing butterflies and exploring enchanted forests.

In her dreams, she leapt through fields of tall grass- the wind blowing through her fur- and played hide-and-seek with her friends under the bright blue sky. Each adventure felt so real, and Luna treasured every moment.

As the stars began to twinkle in the night sky, the soft glow of the moon filtered through the window, casting a gentle light across the room. Luna snuggled deeper into her blanket, feeling safe and content.

Hours passed, but Luna remained in her peaceful slumber, dreaming of all the adventures that awaited her tomorrow. With her heart full of happiness and her spirit renewed, she knew that each new day would bring fresh adventures to explore. And so, in her little corner of the world, Luna the cat slept soundly, embraced by the warmth of her home and the magic of her dreams.

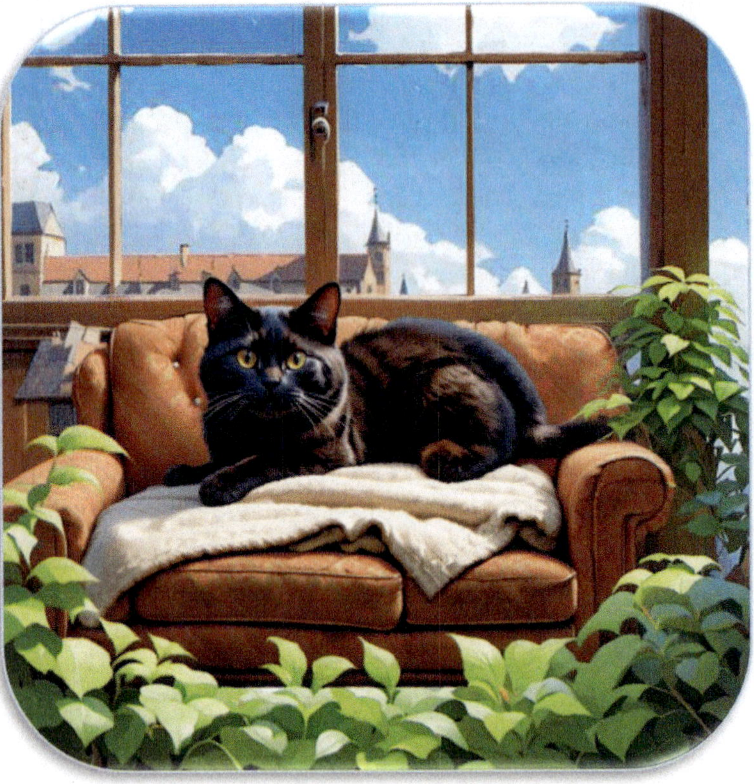

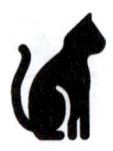

Luna would like to say thank everyone for buying and reading her book and ask you all to be kind to all animals especially us cats.

If you are thinking of getting a cat, please have a rescue one like me so we can have the homes we deserve thank you.

Luna would also like to say thank you to cats' protection for looking after her and helping her find her forever home.

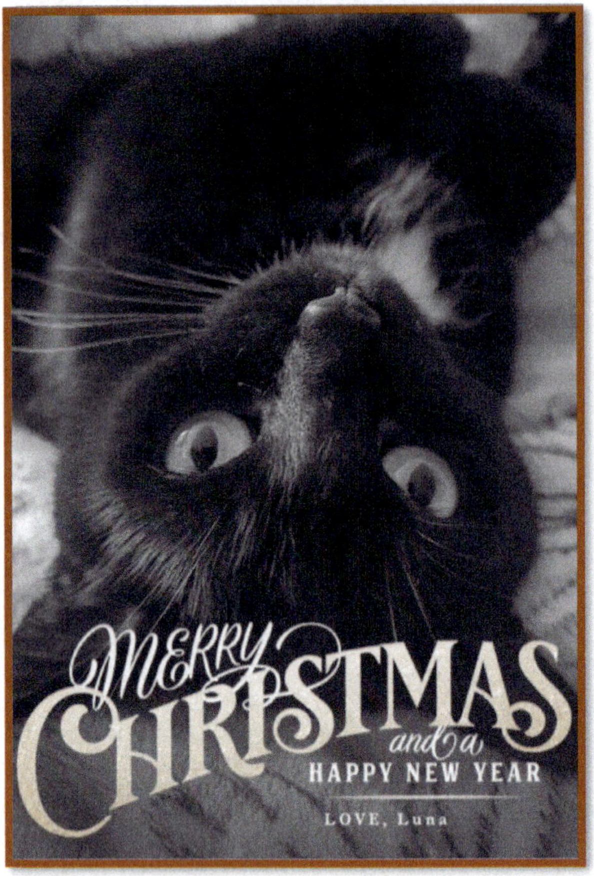
MERRY
CHRISTMAS
and a
HAPPY NEW YEAR
LOVE, Luna

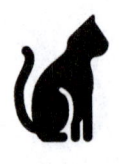

With grateful thanks to David Hall for once again being our editor.